HAWAIIAN SHAMANISM

SECRETS OF THE MODERN SHAMAN
EMPOWER YOURSELF AND CHANGE YOUR LIFE

HAWAIIAN SHAMANISM

SECRETS OF THE MODERN SHAMAN
EMPOWER YOURSELF AND CHANGE YOUR LIFE

Rev. Arlene Phelan Ph.D.

Copyright © 2018 Dr. Arlene Phelan Ph.D.

Hawaiian Shamanism Secrets of the Modern Shaman
Empower Yourself and Change Your Life

All rights reserved. No part of this book may be used or reproduced or transmitted in any form or by any means, electronic or mechanical, including photocopying, recording or by any information storage and retrieval system, without permission in writing from the publisher, except in the case of brief quotations embodied in critical articles and reviews.

Paperback ISBN: 978-1539738824

Publishing & Promotion Services
DM BOOKPRO
EasyBookPublishing.com

DEDICATION

*This book is dedicated to bringing you
Hawaiian Shamanism,
Secrets of the Modern Shaman
to Empower You and Change Your Life*

*With grateful appreciation for inspiration
For the last 40 years of shamanic training
And the sacred Hawaiian teachings from:*

Kahu Serge Kahili King, Kumu Hula Susan Pa'iniu Floyd, Kupuna Nana Veary, Kahuna Abraham Kawaii, Aunty Laura Kealoha Yardley, Po'oKahuna David Kaonohiokala Bray, Kumu Hula Uncle Frank Kawaikapuokalani Hewett, Po'oKahuna Pule Lanakila Brandt and hanai'ed son Michael Yee, the Reverends Melainah Yee, Chris Reid, Rebecca Thompson, Lynn Kaleihaunani Melena and Jan Venturini.

Special appreciation to the many helpers in Spirit,
The Halau and Ka 'Ohana Nui 'O Uli, The family of Uli

My beloved family and friends
My esteemed fellow ministering peers worldwide
Reverend Doti Boon and CCL, San Jose, California
The students and clients whom I serve

Appreciation to the Editors, the Reverends:
Carolyn V. Keyes and Ronald E. McLain, B.Msc.

E Aloha Mana Pono

Blessings of Love, Power and Abundant Good
You all are my Ohana and always a part of me

THE SHAMAN STAR

The seven-pointed star is the Shaman Star. No matter what your tradition or belief, the star (*hoku*) is indeed a magical and wondrous symbol. It is meaningful to me because it preserves the shaman way of those who desire to evolve into a deeply rooted spirituality in the beliefs and practices of higher consciousness and yet, it is much more... As it is in other cultures, the powerful esoteric Hawaiian symbol, goes way beyond shamanism. One of the oldest recorded meanings given to this star is found within the Kabbalistic tradition, where it represents the sphere of Venus and the power of love.

In Christianity, the heptagram or septagram (seven-pointed star) is seen as a symbol of perfection (God) and the seven days of creation. It also conveys the seven gifts of the Holy Spirit: Wisdom, Knowledge, Understanding (insight), Counsel (seer of truth), Fortitude (strength), Reverence (piety), and Awe (Wonder and Fear) of the Lord. In Native American tradition, the symbol represents the seven directions: North, East, West, South, Above, Below, and the Center Within. It also represents seven major native teachings: Truth, Respect, Love, Courage, Honesty, Wisdom, and Humility. At the heart of the esoteric mystery of the seven-pointed star is the knowledge of the spiritual Light at our center and points to the progression of the initiate into mystical wisdom. The heptagram is called the Elven or Faerie Star of Neopagan beliefs. It is identified as the gateway to the Otherworld; each point carries meaning and magick.

The star symbol is found throughout Polynesia. In Hawaii, it is thought to represent the ancestors and Kanaloa, known as the god of the ocean, winds, stars, and the overseer of navigation.

The Shaman Star is like a road map leading the individual toward their desired goal. A critical physical map for the Hawaiian navigator is the knowledge of the celestial spheres to set course and direction. The *hokulea* is a mental Star Compass. It reveals a mental process the mariner uses to plot a course to memory, in the old way, by means of utilizing the navigational stars. The stars provide critical information for the journey. Metaphysically, it is a mental construct to help you remember who you are and what is needed to navigate your star-led path.

The stars (*na hoku*) hold a personal legacy for Hawaiians. Their celestial family is composed of stars and constellations that represent some of Hawaii's greatest chiefs and rulers. Many modern voyagers trace their lineage to the star families. It is a source of comfort that their kupuna (revered elders), and ancestors, are watching over them and guiding them along their journey since ancient times. Today, the seven-pointed star is a symbol that brings into focus the Hawaiian shamanic path and the first seven principles. The star points the way to develop the Shaman Healer Within to be all that they can be.

The star on the cover (*Hoku Malama*) means illuminated body, or causing enlightenment. Radiant illumination (a'o) signifies the secrets of the modern shaman, which can be seen by others even if it is hidden from the conscious mind of the wearer who is seeking to find it. Inside the book, the larger star assists in the mystical navigation through the power (*mana*) of *Hawaiian Shamanism* at the start of each chapter.

The smaller star, placed strategically within the pages, helps you to explore particular navigational points or ideas. The Hawaiian aka rays (spiritual essence) weave in and through the mysteries to entice you to consciously absorb the multi-layers of its mystical empowerment. That which is metaphysically imbued between the lines, nudges you to discover the deeper secrets within yourself to empower and change your life.

Contents

Dedication	V
The Shaman Star	VI
Foreword	XI
Preface	XIII
Introduction	1
Prepare to Read Hawaiian Shamanism	4
Pule Wehe – Opening Prayer Ritual	7

Chapter 1. Hawaiian Shamanism — 9
- Introduction — 10
- Kalakupua – Kupua Tradition — 12
- Lineage of Kupua Shamanism — 14

Chapter 2. Introduction to Mysticism — 18
- Philosophy of Mysticism — 19
- Hawaiian Mysticism — 20

Chapter 3. Ancient Hawaiian Mysteries — 26
- Sacred Mysteries of Mu — 26
- Hawaiian Theosophy – Ho'omana Kahiko — 27
- Po'ohuna - Divine Mysteries — 29
- Po – Understanding the World of Spirit — 30
- Kumulipo — 30
- I'O – Divine Source — 31
- IAO – Principle of Divine Energy — 32
- Uli – Sacred Mother of Creation — 35
- The Pantheon — 36

Chapter 4. Spirits of Humanity — 39
- Hika-Po-Loa – Triumvirate: Kane, Ku and Lono — 39
- Unihipili, Uhane, and Au'makua — 41
- Akua – The Four Gods Kane, Ku, Lono, Kanaloa — 43
- The Triune Person — 46

Chapter 5. The Kahuna — 49
- Po'okahuna – Priests of Divine Mysteries — 51
- Hawaiian Definitions — 53
- Message From a Hawaiian Kahuna — 55
- Teaching - Ho'omana Kahiko and Huna — 56
- The Kahuna Religion — 58

Contents

Chapter 6. Modern Shaman Training — 61
   Introduction – Modern Shaman Training — 62
   Personal Consciousness Development — 63
   Modern Consciousness Values System — 64
   Consciousness Levels 1 – 9 Summary — 65
   The Sacred Bowl of Light — 67
   The Challenge of Personal Growth — 69
   The Practice of Aloha — 72
   Aloha Healing Format — 78

Chapter 7. Modern Shaman Mysticism — 81
   Modern Shaman Initiate – Ho'omaka — 82
   Kupua Transformation — 82
   Shapeshifting — 83

Chapter 8. Shaman Principles — 87
   Introduction to Kupua Shaman Principles — 87
   Qualities of Consciousness — 88
   Operating Kupua Principles — 88
   Ho'omanamana Mystical Process — 95

Chapter 9. Realities of The Kupua — 97
   Ho'omanamana Reality – Creating Realities — 99
   Reality Divisions — 100
   Moving Between Realities — 102

Chapter 10. Mysteries of Mana — 105
   The Ancient Empowerment Practice — 106
   Movement of Mana — 109
   Mana Flow Rules – The Kanawai Akua — 111

Chapter 11. Maintain Mana Flow — 112
   Mana Flow Decisions — 112
   PEMS Mana Disruption Locator — 114
   A. Pono Barometer Chart – Full Mana Flow — 115
   B. Pono Barometer Chart – Moderate Flow — 116
   C. Pono Barometer Chart - Lowest to Empty — 117
   Reconnect to Source — 118
   Kalana Hula Manifesting Meditation Practice — 120

Contents

Chapter 12. Mystical Practices — 123
    Mystical Practices Chart — 124
    Inner Work Discipline – Ulukau and Ike Papalua — 125
    The Eye of Kanaloa — 126
    Connecting with the Shaman Star — 128
    Meditation – No'ono'o — 128
    Walking Meditation — 129
    Expanded Awareness – Hakalau — 130
    HA Breath – Higher Consciousness Access — 131
    Light Alignment – Ho'opololei — 133
    Sacred Sounds — 134
    IAO Chant — 136
    Pule – Effective Prayer Action — 136
    Haipule – Activating Prayer — 137
    Divination - Kilokilo — 138
    Hula – Spiritual Practice — 143
    Ha'a – Sacred Movement — 145
    Temple Healing Practices — 147
    Revelatory Dream – Moe'uhane — 148

Chapter 13. Halau – Angels, Guides, Ancestors — 152
    The Halau Guardians — 152
    Awaiku – Hawaiian Angels — 154
    Spirit – Angels, Guides, and Ancestors — 155
    Communications with the Ancestors — 157

Chapter 14. Work of The Modern Shaman — 160
    The Shaman Mask — 161
    The Practice of Pono - Ka Hana Pono — 162
    Ho'oponopono Basics — 162
    The Internalizing Practice of Ho'oponopono — 166
    The Carriers of the Light — 167

Pule Ho'opau - Closing Ritual — 171
Acknowledgement — 172
Bibliography — 176

Foreword

It is with great delight, I introduce Reverend Arlene Phelan, Ph.D., who dedicates this book to all who are willing and interested in mastering the mysteries of living a great life! Reverend Phelan's lifelong work focused on transformational teachings of Hawaiian Temple Lomi Lomi; channeling elements of Air, Wind, Water, Earth, Plants, Animals, People and Spirit in Temple Kahi Loa sessions; using Ha'a (sacred temple Hula) for healing and empowerment; conducting counseling and support for those in need; writing; lecturing; and leading ministerial preparation programs in Hawaii and the USA mainland.

Always curious to learn more, Arlene continued to study the ancient ways of Hawaiian shamanism and theosophy. She also acquired her doctorate in Metaphysical Counseling, earned the title of Corporate Shaman in a manufacturing company and founded her own professional hospitality financial management consulting firm where she joyfully continued her transformational appointments, and taught workshops all across the United States.

As my teacher, Reverend Phelan taught through humor and by example to help me uncover and discover the secrets of the hidden ancient mana'o deep within, which empowered a great change for the better. Through her teaching, I learned Kupua, which is one who uses the powers of awareness and consciousness, along with the forces of nature, to harmonize physical, emotional, mental and spiritual relationships in all situations.

In order to understand deeply the Hawaiian Aloha ways and mystical teaching of the Kupua, she taught that one must first approach with respect, humbly, withholding judgment, and then listen closely to your own inner knowingness, for it is there that you can access truth. It is in this attitude of acceptance and allowing, that I invite you to read this amazing book. As you read it, you will also automatically enter into the transformational energy of the Halau, where all forces for good gather on the etheric plane to assist in expanding your own mystical knowledge. While you continue to read, just as Reverend Phelan helped me to connect to the higher dimensions, you too may also sense this extended network of support and you may even allow yourself to communicate with these multidimensional beings of good, for they are already guiding forces in your life.

I encourage you to be aware when you enter the mystical energy and attune your senses to all the help that is available to you to go deeper into your own inner knowing. The shaman's way is a dramatic and mystical version of what happens to all of us, if we are willing to live an extraordinary life.

With Deep Reverence, Aloha!
Reverend Rebecca Thompson
Founder of TAGA
Transformation Angels, Guides and Ancestors

Preface

Hawaiian Shamanism is presented from the perspective of the modern shaman connecting to the ancient wisdom teachings. It is the golden thread within it that connects to the very highest essence, and is expressed through *aloha* (love) the code of life and *pono* (righteousness) love in action, which emphasizes the value of the integrity, of rightness, harmony and balance. Sharing the fullness of loving is the vital empowerment (*ho'omana*) that attracts the modern healer, and is why most are drawn to add this ancient Hawaiian knowledge to expand their present wheelhouse.

> "A Shaman is an ordinary person who has chosen to live an extraordinary life by consciously connecting to the Divine with the expressed purpose to create love demonstrated in behavior and in service."

The *Hawaiian Shamanism* material was formally presented as an intensive course August 4, 2013, at the Center for Creative Living in San Jose, California, to people just like you, as a guide to unfolding the empowerment of the Kupua transformational path. It was called, *"The Kupua Shaman Personal Operating Manual, A Guide for Study and Transformation."*

My intention in writing this book is to simply share my mana'o (my thinking) with aloha. The goal is to help you discover the secrets of love (the shaman practices) that are hidden deep within, which can empower you and change your life, if you let it ... and because there once was a little girl (me) who was a shaman ... but didn't know it. She didn't go to a shaman school – didn't live in Hawaii then ... and there was no Hogwarts School of Witchcraft and Wizardry that would have attracted her away from a traditional ministry.

Through it all, her life unfolded in pretty amazing ways as her innate shaman abilities kept "slipping out" ... surprising her many times over. Along the way she heard Father Charlie Moore speak about Jesus being the greatest shaman who ever lived. This planted seeds within her that shamanism is honored in many different belief systems - even in Christianity. It is for all people, for all lifetimes. So, here we are today, graced with the knowledge that it's ok to have magic in your life! I am excited to be revealing the secrets of the modern shaman. It all begins with the journey and the magic that happens along the way, doesn't it? Starting in the later part of my life, accepting greater vistas and opening to opportunities, dramatic change began to take place by accepting the gift and with understanding the meaning of the shaman shoes.

The story of the shaman shoes unfolded after I had been bombarded, it seemed, from all sides to accept the mastery role in my newly founded Hawaiian Lomi Lomi practice. Not quite standing confident under public scrutiny, I retreated to continue registering for more advanced Lomi Lomi and additional shamanic instruction. Inevitably the gift of the shaman shoes turned up while I was packing to go to another training. My story:

> "A Hawaiian friend gave me a pair of very flashy orange sandals. On first sight, I thought, 'Whoa, these are so bright, they must be shoes for a shaman!' As my conservative nature sounded alarms, I thanked her and not wanting to hurt her feelings, discreetly tucked them away in my suitcase vowing, 'They aren't 'quite right' for me.' One day during Kupua training, I participated in a little-known manifesting ritual called *Ku Pono*. It strengthens confidence in having the right, the desire, the will and the power to manifest what you desire. My intention was to develop my own Kupua 'mastery.' I am forever grateful to my Kupono partner, Guido for his assistance. It worked. I instantly had the power and confidence to succeed. Needless to say, it was the day I took the shoes out of my suitcase (newly found shaman bag). I was committed; that day I put on my shaman shoes. I actually wore those bright orange sandals in service all over Hawaii. Lol!"

What is important for you to know is, that *you have shaman shoes* waiting for you! The shoes are a symbol which hold the secrets for the modern shaman; you can be empowered to change your life in ways you cannot imagine. Please follow me as I reveal what I have learned.

Rev. Arlene Phelan, Ph.D.

INTRODUCTION

As interest in self-development grows, more people are attracted to Hawaiian Shamanism, which reflects the value of understanding the ancient use of *Aloha* (love), *Mana* (power) and *Pono* (loving action). This links into the ability modern spiritual seekers have to quickly comprehend and open to the same universal truths Kahu Lanakila Brandt outlines:

> "Ancient teachings contain eternal truths. You must reinterpret them for today's world, combine the most vital elements of both periods and translate them into an effective force in your life."

This mystical information is written to connect you to the modern application of the ancient path. *Hawaiian Shamanism* is instruction for contemporary living, based on the sacred teachings for the ordinary person who feels drawn to explore a deeper, more empowering life. It can also be a personal operating manual for walking in the "shaman shoes," which is found first and foremost in the influence from the lineage of Lemuria and Uli, and through the teachings of various ancient and modern Kahuna.

Secrets Of The Modern Shaman invites you, whether you are an ordinary person, student, or a practicing shaman, to gain knowledge, expand your horizon, or just be immersed in the empowering source that "goes to the bone" deep within yourself where the High Self flourishes. It is this very sacred base and the Hawaiian principles that provide mana/power and connects you with insightful Hawaiian belief systems.

There is a "call" to unfold the contemporary mystic within yourself; to know the ability you have is the same as the ancients knew, loved and lived. It is a dramatic and metaphysical version of what happens to all of us. As the shaman archetype is becoming activated in the collective consciousness, people are becoming aware that they have the capacity to be a master and the very real potential that they may become a modern shaman who functions in the mystical empowerment as does the Hawaiian Kahuna Kupua.

Shamanic instruction is consciousness expansive. It will tease your senses and at times be confusing. The shaman world stretches your mind; and entices you to go beyond your understanding; it requires using your intuition or your *Uhikau* (Divine inspiration) interpretive abilities. The same way unexplained supernatural interpretive powers can be divinely given to a person, so knowledge and understanding can come to the person who makes the effort to read the language and words of ancient and modern Hawaiian Shamanism. The message just may be tucked in shaman shoes that await your investigation.

The Lineage of the Teaching

Many direct quotes from teachers are used in this book so that you sense the heart of the master and can validate the findings in keeping with your own inner wisdom. To say that this work is entirely based on Hawaiian or Polynesian traditions is not entirely true; my spiritual and intellectual understanding and interpretations through mediumship influenced it greatly. The different sources called upon to produce this particular version of *Hawaiian Shamanism,* pull from each contributor's shamanic path. It provides many different pieces of the puzzle to form a valuable modern collective point of reference. The teaching is expressed to introduce those who are from different cultural backgrounds to be open to the deep beliefs of Hawaiian thinking that we know and revere.

It is the spiritually awakened modern Metaphysician who may come the closest jn conveying the mystical link of the Hawaiian core. This metaphysical lineage is expressed through the *Halau*

Guardians (the many Kahuna who are the ancient ones), and in the reincarnation of the souls who are dedicated to bringing their wisdom and mana to people around the world. The enlightening mana of the Hawaiian legacy permeates the world today because of the dedicated lives of the Kahuna priests of the past and those who lived it. The *Aloha Spirit* is conveyed from their work as they continue their mission in the afterlife as transforming angels, guides and ancestors. Both physically birthed Hawaiians and those who channel their energy and teaching, as well as those great masters who are reincarnated as the mystics of our time, carry the light and their work forward. This is the energy of enlightenment, which emerges in the form of modern day insight.

The world is seeking this empowerment, which results in *Pono* - the perfection of loving action that all spiritually evolving communities desire. This spurs us into seeking the higher truths of *Ho'omana* (Hawaiian spirituality), which changes thinking and transforms lives.

> "The future belongs to the Individual who takes up the innate commitment to step out of its cocoon or nest and soar into a new realm of possibilities."
>
> - Kahu Abraham Kawaii

Prepare to Read Hawaiian Shamanism

Step into the mystical wisdom of Hawaiian Shamanism with heartfelt preparation. In the Hawaiian way, each person always connects with Divine Source before beginning the day or beginning a task. Every activity starts with prayer or pule (pronounced pull ay). Note that the modern shaman may use different words, phrases, affirmations, prayers or mantras than the ancients; it is the thoughts in your mind and spoken words that emphasize and produce the manifestation of your intent. Let your inner shaman teacher become a participant to link with Source to join in dedication of this book for higher purpose with a ritual written by my very dear friend Lynn Kaleihaunani Melena, of Big Island, Hawaii, to bring blessings for you and these teachings. Connect with the ancients by using both the English and Hawaiian words in the rituals and throughout the book.

The Hawaiian language contains vibrational encoding. Actually, the Hawaiian is a language of higher consciousness vibrations and feelings. The subtlety of the true Hawaiian language is delivered through the layers of meaning in each syllable. Ultimately, each layer of meaning depends on the subtle sound of the consciousness of the speaker and the nuances of the oral tradition. Even when you don't know the meaning of the words, vowels in and of themselves transmit consciousness in sound, and convey meaning that the Shaman prayerfully structures. For example: The special vowels within *IAO* (Ee-Ah-Oh) are the most sacred sounds in the Hawaiian language. The consonants frame specific thought movement and weave in appropriate rhythm, and pause the senses for absorption of the energy being expressed.

To ensure this consciousness transmission, it is the rule that every word and syllable must end in a vowel, so that no two consonants are ever heard without a vowel sound between them.

Hawaiian was an oral language and did not become written until Western missionaries arrived, translating it based primarily on bending sounds to fit the English language sounds of five vowels and 8 consonants. Diacritical marks called ʻokina or kahako were used to designate the nuance of sound. In this publication, I have tried to use the correct Hawaiian spelling. However, due to the constraint of my word program, use of the native diacritical marking is not always possible. I apology for this limitation, for I realize that missing the ʻokina or kahakō can change not only how a word sounds, but also its basic meaning. To overcome this limitation, I have inserted the appropriate translation of Hawaiian words where possible. In addition, it is much easier to read Hawaiian words if you know a few pronunciation rules of the Hawaiian ʻalepapeka (alphabet) and the rhythm of the syllables. Understanding both will give you a sense of the Hawaiian consciousness imbedded within the words and phrases.

Vowels					**Consonants**					
A	**E**	**I**	**O**	**U**	**H**	**K**	**L**	**M**	**N**	**P** **W**
Ah	Ay	Ee	Oh	Oo	Hay	Kay	Lah	Moo	Noo	Pee Vay

The Hawaiian vowels are "vocalized" as outlined:

Vowel Pronunciation Guide

    A Sound: **Ah** as in jaw, law
    E Sound: **Ay** as in way
    I Sound: **Ee** as in we
    O Sound: **Oh** as in whole
    U Sound: **Oo** as in new, renew

Syllable Pronunciation Guide

- Words may start with any letter, vowel or consonant
- Words never end with a consonant

- Syllables in words are only one or two letters, never longer
- Syllables must end with a vowel, or can be a single vowel, but can never be a single consonant

Intone the Hawaiian words in slow, rhythmic phrasing as you would in sounding a chant. Use the pronunciation guide for thoughtful expression and for syllable distinction. Example:

E Po'e Au'makua. Say: **Ay Poh ay   Ah Oo mah kOo ah**
Na Ohana. Say: **Nah Oh hah nah**

Vowels are consciousness. Words are groupings of consciousness that carry power and meaning; the energy is part of the life force (*mana*), which can heal or kill us. Since words are transmitted consciousness, extending your sound vibration a little longer on vowels or at the end of a word extends the transmission of consciousness of the thought. Notice when you use sounds in this fashion that you actually are in touch with the deeper power of the Hawaiian word or phrase. In addition, attention to the meaning of the English words will also take on the deeper spirituality the vowels transmit.

The pule uses the word *Ohana* (family) and invokes the mana of *our Ohana* and at the same time, acknowledges ourselves as *Divine Selves* present. Ohana (family deeply related) exemplifies family and spiritual connectedness. It is not just a biological family, but also the deeper spiritual connection of the relationship. You are one of us. We are one with you. We are one together in the *Universal Ohana*. As this relates to reading *Hawaiian Shamanism*, may you feel yourself as a member of the Hawaiian family unit to understand the beliefs and practices as a part of your legacy that includes and serves you in the modern world today.

Sense your own consciousness as you read each phrase of the Pule in both Hawaiian and English. You may literally feel a sensation of sacred presence that supports your intentions, as it once did for the ancient Hawaiian priests who wove consciousness into their rituals. Feel yourself as an intimate part (oneness) with the tone being set to receive the Hawaiian knowledge and understand how it relates to you in your life today.

Pule Wehe - Opening Prayer Ritual

E Po'e Au'makua
We call forth and connect to Divine Source, our parent God that dwells within
Na Ohana our Spirit Family,
Na Kahuna the Masters from the stillness within,
Na Kupuna beloved ancestors, guides and teachers
E We call forth
Ho'olohe We listen in deep sincerity
E ko'u pule We call forth our sacred prayer

We call forth this space to be blessed and make sacred this place for understanding *Hawaiian Shamanism and the Secrets of the Modern Shaman* to empower and change our life. We create within our Selves readiness to receive the Divine Love and Essence that is within each one of us.

We open ourselves to these things so that deeper guidance may be received. We call forth and establish within ourselves the emotional, mental and physical groundedness and center ourselves. In our effort today we use this guidance in a way that is profound and useful in our lives.

We honor our ancestors, past, present, and future, as well as our teachers and guides, and ask that they step into our consciousness at this time.

(Take a moment to notice their presence and acknowledge them into our presence).

We ask for the presence of our Au'makua, our spirit Godparents, to assist us in taking these higher energies and grounding them into our bodies so we may take action in our lives. Guide and lead us on our journey.

(Notice their presence and acknowledge them).

We invite our Ohana, our soul family who have been with us since the beginning of our soul's evolution. Some are with us in this lifetime, but many are in the spirit world watching and supporting us.

(Be aware of their presence and acknowledge them).

Finally, we acknowledge our Divine Selves.

(As you do this, feel your heart opening and increasing the capacity to love).

We set forth the intention that all these energies blend and assist in our growth. We ask to be clear channels and be loving mentors to hold space for all today, so this may be of personal value and service to the world. Help us to connect with like-minded souls. Bless our work and help us to use this time wisely together. We in turn, send our blessings.

E Aloha Mana Pono
The blessings of Love, Empowerment and Right Action.

Amama ua noa.
The prayer is complete. All sacred prohibitions have been lifted.

Mahalo, Mahalo, Mahalo.
Thank you! Thank you! Thank you!
May the breath of life stay with you.

Chapter 1. Hawaiian Shamanism

To know Hawaiian shamanism, you must consider the foundation of the Hawaiians of old before the introduction of the Ali'i system and the constructs of the Western and Eastern ways. We look to Polynesian history (*mo'olelo*). Mo'olelo carries meanings in the story telling that are sometimes unexplainable. It provides us with the shamanic traditions and reveals insight through the myths that depict multilayered relationships in the oneness (*lokahi*) of all life. We thoughtfully enter the world of Hawaiian culture rich in tradition, knowledgeable in protocol, and whose daily life is integrated with Hawaiian spirituality (*ho'omana*). Ho'omana Kahiko is the indigenous materialistic spirituality, which provides the basis to know the thoughts and beliefs (*mana'o i'o*) of the people. Aunty Pilahi Paki, known as the Keeper of the Secrets of Hawaii, placed the importance of Hawaiian knowledge on "thinking Hawaiian." Aunty Paki said:

> "If you 'think Hawaiian' regardless of the language you use, it will be the language of *Aloha* and *Aloha* is the language, which reveals the connection to all people.

To be able to "think Hawaiian" requires a dedicated focus that becomes effortless discipline and practice, which accesses a deeper level of awareness in stored consciousness of both the individual and collective humanity if one is to reap the rewards of Aloha, resulting in pono (living righteously) in the family and in the community.

Introduction

Today, we see Hawaiian shamanism as being comprised of many schools of thought derived from different orders and priesthood lineages of ancient wisdom and practices. In the past, all systems were handed down orally from generation to generation-through family traditions and community life. It is important to seek to be introduced to the real values of Hawaiian shamanism that emanates from the wellspring of the heart and soul of the people. This ancient loving philosophy is beautifully expressed on the web pages of Kahu Kahealani Kawaiolamanaloa Satchitananda:

> "Being Hawaiian is not just about a race of people or the koko. It is about the spiritual nobility of the soul, the living legacy of love/aloha and the creative power/mana of manifestation that the ancestors gifted to us and left for us to uphold. It's about a state of heart, a state of mind, a state of consciousness of good, and a state of oneness. We uphold this gift by understanding, contemplating and being Pono, walking in the footsteps of na kupuna, na ancestors and na 'aumakua in alignment with the Divine/Ke Akua and in harmonious relations. All of humanity can benefit from these ancient cultural values of spiritual nobility, a way of Seeing, a way of Being, the Sacred Hawaiian Way in the Spirit of Pure Aloha."

Note: Ko means of you. Koko means the bloodlines.

The truth spoken by Kahu Kahealani is a shared living legacy now encapsulated in a very spiritual profoundness in our collective consciousness. We realize that we are esoterically an integral part. Now made available physically to the world, the teachings literally expand the world consciousness through classes, books, online access and residential programs. As an indigenous culture, religious practices evolved in different ways over time and from place to place throughout Polynesia. Unifying (*lokahi*) with the deep and genuine reverence for life in all respects (personal, family, community and the land) comprises the essence of its religion and theosophy. Life was a mission concerned with living pono (loving right action, righteousness), demonstrating aloha (love, respect, honor), mana (spiritual power), and the practice of kokua (helping) formed by insightful religious beliefs. This creates love demonstrated in behavior and in service. Hawaiian author Pali Jae Lee writes in *Tales of The Night Rainbow:*

> "During these ancient times, the only religion was one of family and oneness with all things. The people were in tune with nature, plants, trees, animals, the 'aina, and each other."

They believed in the unity and the inter-connectedness of all things. All are integrally linked to each other creating a sound body of intellect with a strong, solid spiritual pono foundation. Lokahi is the great unity honoring all things sacred and the sacredness in all things behind these three major forces, which make up the universe in the oneness as they experienced it:

1. Spiritual forces
2. Humankind and all living creatures
3. The environment and all natural resources

By maintaining unity among all forces, lokahi restores mind, body, and spirit. Out of reverence and respect comes a natural caring for all things and all people. This creates and restores pono (loving right action) and all it embraces. Aunty Laura Kealoha Yardley defines the qualities of pono behavior in *Ancient Memories 2001*:

> "Goodness, uprightness, morality, moral qualities, correct or proper procedures, protocol, excellence, well-being, prosperity, benefit, behalf, equity, sake, true condition of nature, duty; moral fitting, beneficial, successful, proper order, accurate, correct. To treat with respect, we often must choose to remain silent rather than speak prematurely and possibly in error. We choose our words carefully in order to avoid hurting others unnecessarily. This is strength and requires much internal processing. Sometimes we come away with answers, and sometimes we come away with more questions."

Hawaiians of old believed the spirit of God, whatever form it takes, is inside everyone and everything. In the opportunities to practice pono, the ancient wisdom is one of learning through the circumstances of life. The values of the people became the desired rules in social conduct. The first and foremost principle is God connection with the social wisdom and value of Aloha. Aloha is a view of life, a state of mind and heart; the foundation for Hawaiian life. People attempted to treat others with much care for the spirit of god dwelling within. In particular, they generously shared their hospitality with all, including strangers.

Through the spiritual understanding that god is ever-present, the social action overrides individual greed and gain. The welfare of others becomes more important than personal gratification. By realizing that one's survival and welfare are dependent upon a harmonious relationship with other people, places and objects, one is led to demonstrate aloha through harmonious actions and nonviolence. When you understand aloha, you treat everyone with the responsibility of being a guiding light for one another. It becomes a call to service for everyone to serve one another.

Kalakupua – Kupua Tradition

Hawaiian Shamanism is a metaphysical, earth-based spiritual tradition called Kalakupua. This is the introduction to the mystical aspects, which stem from ancient times. The first layer of meaning for Kalakupua is:

> Kala means: to untie, unbind and set free
> Kupua means: to create magic

The deeper mystical aspects of Kalakupua explain the mystery and magic attributed to the Kupua practice and practitioner. The root of Kalakupua in *Melville's Esoteric Hawaiian Dictionary:*

Kala is:
1. to liberate, free, release from bondage, untie, forgive, pardon, excuse.
2. to support with defense, uphold, lend help, aid, succor, comfort, strengthen, energize, assist, sustain, keep from sinking or falling.
3. to proclaim, announce, make an announcement; issue a proclamation, publish officially.
4. expression used by the ancients when they prayed to their gods for forgiveness for themselves and others.

Ka' la' is: a radiation of light from the sun.

Kupu is:
1. to come from the highest.
2. to emerge from a shell or an egg and expand into life, to grow or sprout from a seed and develop and grow.
3. an offspring or product of.
4. a Spirit, supernatural being, in reference to Deity.
5. to emerge from a godly being, emanation from spirit.

A is:
1. of, pertaining to, from, indicating source, derivation.
2. to, belonging to; connected with a person, place, time or thing; related unto.

The background of Kalakupua first draws attention to the properties of magic and mystery. Connecting to the ancient shamanic source reveals the infinite secrets of empowerment and identifies not only the mission, describes the work, and it also calls into recognition the individual as the core mystical conveyance of Hawaiian Shamanism. Today, the ancient Hawaiian mystical shamanic practice of Kalakupua is called Kupua. To shorten the word fits into the modern trend. However, let us always link into the mystical depth and meaning of the full empowerment that the kala root implies. Investigating the ancient metaphysical origin of Kupua reveals another contributing influence from the Pantheon of Hawaiian gods. The mystical lineage of Kupua is found within the very composition of the Pantheon consciousness itself. Kahu Lanakila defined this deity connection in *Hawaiian Theosophy, Po'ohuna* (1997):

> "Kupua is one of the lesser gods in the Pantheon."

The modern Kupua tradition carries this ancient mana. At the same time, the profound roots of the lineage must be an integral part of the Kupua mana and the transformative work. Kahu Serge King provides further insight to the historic lineage of his Kupua path:

> "The Kupua in its purest sense is derived from ancient records of the Kupua as a shapeshifter in Asian and in Polynesian cultures. The Hawaiian Kupua refers to a specialized healer who works with the powers of the mind and the forces of nature. In that respect, it is very similar to the Siberian Tungusic word 'Shaman.' Kahuna Kupua is described as Master of Spirits; Mystic or Shaman."

The Lineage of Kupua Shamanism

Honoring the lineage of Kupua Shamanism is an important step in developing a strong spiritual foundation. Of his personal lineage, Serge says:

> "I was trained in a traditional way in 'Kalakupua,' or 'Kupua' for short, a near equivalent to 'shamanism,' by my Auntie Laka and my Uncle Wana of the Kahili family, who originally came from Kauai. I was hanai'ed into that family as the grandson of Joseph Kahili in 1957. My last teacher, Wana Kahili, granted me the title of "Kahuna Kupua" in 1975."

The Kahuna Kupua tradition establishes a legacy of spiritual nobility, love and power for Mind, Body and Spirit. It is up to the initiate to discover it and own it. The mystical path of the Kahuna Kupua awakens into Oneness/Lokahi, and the true Spirit of Aloha. The deeds of the Kupua are the gifts to everyone. It is an ancient empowering path of shared spirituality, that brings a much-needed healing for people, our planet, and us through the inspiration of the Kupua.

Esoterically, the lineage is more than just information about your birth and your ancestors. It is also about the path you build with the sole purpose of creating a legacy for the future. The modern lineage of the Kahuna Kupua is one of initiation open to all cultures. It is introduced into the lineage and legacy of the world. One of the great challenges of accepting the ancient lineage from the Hawaiian Shamanism spiritual tradition called Kalakupua is the power it bestows upon the initiate. It requires that you must overcome your deepest fear or doubt, not that you are inadequate but that within yourself, you are most powerful beyond measure.

The Mystical Kupua Shaman

The mystically trained Kupua Shaman connects with the Divine to know and sense Truth, to move and shift energies, empower individuals and have the power to make changes in their own life. The Kupua teachings I have received include mysteries and mediumistic dimensions. It is a combination of Hawaiian lessons from both physical and Spirit instructors who embrace the Aloha Way.

The Kupua is an ordinary person who has the ability to connect with God and is a healer who has made a choice to do good, that transforms the ordinary into the extraordinary. He or she is seen as one who possesses knowledge of the inner world and uses that knowledge to live the power and principles in everyday life. They use innate knowledge in the context of present social and cultural environment; thus, the primary quality of a shaman is a healer of souls in all walks of life. Further insights define the Kupua as a Shaman who:

- Functions from the perspective of principles, not rigid dogmas or limitations
- Weaves in and out of the discernable realities
- Is consciously aware of their own views but able to help others expand different perspectives
- Can be effective in every aspect of life

What Does It Mean, "To Have Kupua?"

Mystery surrounds the world of the Kupua. The question is, "What does it mean, to have Kupua?" In ancient and modern times myths abound from many cultures that have their own Kupua. Some stories are fairytale-like legends that tell about amazing transformations and others are like documentaries that explain the natural world. Kupua sometimes appear as a person and sometimes as an animal, vegetable or mineral form, and they always possess supernatural powers. Many stories described them as either tricksters or vindictive monsters that create havoc and destroy or devour their victims. Other myths depict Kupua as kindly spirits who give watchful care to the members of their own families. Religious beliefs, societal influence and personal experience add flair and influence concepts about them. Together they contribute to an accurate overall portrait of how the mystical personality develops within the individual. Deeper metaphysical truth may provide insight into Hawaiian myths, that if one "has Kupua," one has magical powers.

At the root of the matter, is that Kupua are part human and part god, having a dual nature. The human part is seen as a result of an animal ancestry, which still resides along with their Divinity. According to Hawaiian Kumukahi educators, Kamapua'a is one of the best-known Kupua *"he kino papalua"* (a dual-formed person). He has kinolau, or many body forms, "human sides and dimensional depth." Kamapua'a can show that he or she is a man or a pig and can take the form of a fish or plant body. This knowledge reminds us that nature has a wild side, sometimes destructive and other times, thoughtful, productive and loving. The stories emphasize the need for conserving natural resources. We can see the Divine strengths and human faults in him. As people, we can see that we have many similar strengths and multiple faults as well.

Mo'o holds the key to the deepest, nearly forgotten magic. Mo'o means lizard or gecko, and like the chameleon, they have ability to transform. The greatest mo'o are known as "dragons," from which you learn to be a guardian. As such, you must accept the responsibility to protect people, the water (representing mana), resources, and everything that comes to drink of it. The myths also tell of the kindness and nurturing or about mean and punishing characteristics. The stories remind us of the struggle within all people to come from their highest nature. In the outer world, it cautions that it is always best to ask first before taking something that belongs to another or entering someone else's place. Mo'o presence alerts recognition of the mysteries of phenomena. If you are especially attentive, mo'o will share healing secrets and how to use duality, which resides within all as strength. Through Kupua mo'o mana, you learn how to defeat fear and enter into the sacred place of enlightenment to serve humanity.

Maui is another type of Kupua. He is a demigod in human form. He has a powerful human form only and no other kinolau (body). Maui can do things other men cannot. Although small in stature, like a superhero, he is able to outsmart his opponents. His deeds benefit himself, his family and the greater population. Maui's stories are fantastic and stretch your imagination. They inspire people to attempt heroic and seemingly impossible deeds. Kupua teach important lessons and connect with ka po'e kahiko (the people of old), to help the world better understand and improve the connection of kanaka (people) and nature. Maui demonstrates the right use of mana.

When the question, "What does it mean, to have Kupua?" is answered through the understanding of Hawaiian theosophy, more of the Kupua mana (life force) is revealed. The spiritually advanced Kupua uses inner power to balance with all forces of Nature. The components of all substances combine to manifest in all dimensions and correlate all energy together to create magic. In the sense of the personal power of the modern Kupua Shaman, to "Have Kupua." is to actually "Be Kupua" (the Divine) within the self. You may choose to view Kupua as just a traditional title or pull from the deeper core to unfold the greater mystical potential.

Chapter 2. Introduction to Mysticism

Every time you have a flash of inspiration, a noble thought, a good intention, you are functioning in the mystical state. Mysticism is the normal part of yourself that although it supports everything you perceive, you take no notice of it until you are faced with one of life's problems. Webster defines mysticism as: "Seeking to solve the mysteries of existence by internal illumination." In other words, mysticism is going beyond the externals of life to seek the truth within. It is the practice that will put you into, and remain in direct relation with God, the Absolute, or any unifying principle of life.

> "In mysticism that love of truth, which we saw as the beginning of all philosophy leaves the merely intellectual sphere, and takes on the assured aspect of a personal passion. Where the philosopher guesses and argues, the mystic lives and looks; and speaks, consequently, the disconcerting language of first-hand experience, not the neat dialectic of the schools. Hence whilst the Absolute of the metaphysicians remains a diagram - impersonal and unattainable - the Absolute of the mystics is lovable, attainable, alive."
>
> - Evelyn Underhill
> *Mysticism: A Study in the Nature
> And Development of Spiritual Consciousness*

Philosophy of Mysticism

"A mystic is not a mysterious person; but is one who has a deep, inner sense of Life and Unity with the Whole; mysticism and mystery are entirely different things; one is real while the other may, or may not, be an illusion. There is nothing mysterious in the Truth, so far as It is understood; but all things, of course, are mysteries until we understand them. A mystic is one who intuitively perceives Truth and who, without mental process, arrives at Spiritual Realizations. It is from the teachings of the great mystics that the best in the philosophy of the world has come."

- Ernest Surtleff Holmes
The Science of Mind, Lesson 5: The Perfect Whole

Mysticism is frequently defined as an experience of direct communion with God, or union with the Absolute. The experience may be one of emotional sensing or intellectual thought, which may be felt as a profound shift of realization and belief expansion. Some mystical characteristics are:

1. Ineffability: inability to capture the experience in ordinary language.
2. Ultimate reality or God: immediate consciousness of the transcendent.
3. Noetic quality: mystical experiences reveal an otherwise hidden or inaccessible knowledge.
4. Unity of opposites: sense of oneness, wholeness or completeness.
5. Timelessness: the sense that mystical experiences transcend time/space.
6. A belief in the existence of realities: beyond perceptual or intellectual apprehension.
7. A feeling of encountering the true self: a sense that the experience reveals the nature of our true selves.
8. Cosmic self: one that is beyond life and death, beyond difference and duality, and beyond ego and selfishness.

Mystical Unfoldment

Since the mystic intuitively senses reality and instinctively knows the truth, mystical expertise is unfolded because of experiencing events with metaphysical understanding. Mystical practices lead to spiritual initiation into the deeper soul mysteries of a Living Presence. Because of the very nature of mysticism, the initiates must learn by experiencing for themselves as they embark on a conscious path, which brings transformation through spiritual expansion. The five developmental stages of mysticism are outlined by Evelyn Underhill in *Practical Mysticism*. Not all mystics go through all stages or experience them in the order presented in the pursuit of Kupua development:

1. **Awakening** is the stage where one begins to have some *consciousness of the Absolute or Divine Reality*.

2. **Purgation** is characterized by an awareness of one's own imperfections and finiteness. The response in this stage is one of self-discipline and mortification.

3. **Illumination** is achieved by artists and visionaries as well as being the final stage for some mystics. It is marked by a consciousness of a transcendent order and/or a vision of a new heaven and a new earth.

4. **Complete Purification** is a stage of surrender to the hidden purposes of the *Divine Will* and "unselfing" step.

5. **Union with the One Reality** is the final stage of union with the object of love, the one Reality, God.

Hawaiian Mysticism

There are many definitions of Hawaiian mysticism, but few mention the innermost beliefs. Most describe what mystics *do* rather than talk about what they *believe,* or reveal their deep Spirit link. The mystical perspective of the ancient Hawaiian cultural tradition perceives that God and I and you and I, and you and God and I, are all One. Philosophically, Hawaiian mysticism supersedes the Western assumption that God and I and you and I are ultimately separate and distinct from each other. The ancients ascribed to the teaching through the experience of oneness - a sense of God as aspects of Hika-Po-Loa (the God-head) and as an individuation of Spirits (layered consciousness) that is alive, permeate, and are in the oneness of everything. The people believed that there is no separation – God is all there is. This principle is seen as the weaving of the aka threads connecting all parts of the Creator; all life is founded on love and everything has mana (God power) in it. These beliefs offer a multifaceted sense of mysticism and connectivity throughout all of life.

A profound level of belief emerges through the mystical teaching of *Ho'omanamana*, which means creating with spiritual power. On a deeper level, ho'omanamana means "How to make reality of Divine power." This speaks to the very essence of Hawaiian mysticism, which you will hear about throughout this book in the philosophical thinking, teaching and the practices of gathering, maintaining, and using mystical empowerment. Working at this level naturally moves into the deeper awareness of mystical understanding and customs, which relate to the knowledge and practices that were kept secret until the initiate was ready and committed to using them for higher purpose.

At the heart of the old teachings, ho'omanamana, is aloha (literally - we breathe together), which offers a basis for creating the higher consciousness mana (power) needed for the spiritually evolving Kupua Shaman practitioner. The seed of empowerment grows from the attitude, state of reality and practice of Lokahi (unity of oneness), which is a way of focusing and gathering energy into one point for the purpose of creating life and healing.

> "Some consider it magic because it works with unseen forces, which are nevertheless real, and it produces results not fully understood by some."
>
> – Laura Kealoha Yardley
> *The Heart of Huna* (38)

The esoteric Kahuna continues to teach mystically from the world of Spirit. If you seek the way of the Kupua and link to the ancient po'ohuna, your connection with the universe will be expanded by the beliefs preserved in the keys to Hawaiian theosophy. These beliefs include mystical teaching from the Kumulipo, the Divine Triad and knowledge of the ancestors.

The Mystical Mission of The Kupua

The mystical mission of the Kupua is outlined in the Hawaiian Pantheon. One who has been initiated as a Kupua mystic opens to the empowering knowledge (*mana'o*) of the Kupua lineage in order to have the capacity to work with any and in all expressions of consciousness, which appear appropriately empowering for service to humanity. A Kupua is a healer who uses the powers of mind and the forces of Nature to harmonize physical, emotional, mental and spiritual relationships in all situations.

It is the role of the Kupua to function in the simplicity of aloha - to be in harmony with the Great Power coming from sincerity, spontaneity and with sensitivity to the higher consciousness energy of the heart. The thought processes the Kupua uses, are the same that human beings have used at different stages of development in order to understand and utilize the realm of the ultimate reality for practical living. Thus, the Kupua functions from many different wisdom levels. Kupua knowledge has to do with:

- Awareness of, and the ability to connect with higher energies of the Divine
- The ability to connect with the earth energies and people, places, and things
- Directing powers of mind, and forces of nature
- Connecting to and empowering the aspects of selves through integration and expansion
- Conducting public ceremony and personal rituals
- Mastering the levels of consciousness, realities, and using them in practices of healing
- Connecting to, and using all forms of energies

Kupua Mystical Shamanic Practice

The basis of mystical shamanic practice is that the practitioner wakes up to Divine Consciousness to use the spiritual energy (*Ike*) to create the world he or she envisions. The longer you can consistently focus upon the goal you want, your attention on intention will manifest what you concentrate on. Everything in your awareness is a reflection of your own beliefs. What is perceived to be "true" is only your experience viewed through your own filters of what you call truth. Perception is projection. It is important to realize that any unwanted energies are simply unresolved issues embedded at any level that you are holding from past experience. When your beliefs change, your old perception about your experience is no longer needed to interpret the incident. As your awareness is expanded, you release what no longer fits your new beliefs.

> "The Kupua learns quickly and effectively to view ordinary reality in non-ordinary ways, to recognize non-ordinary events in ordinary circumstances, and to create new circumstances. Life then becomes a marvelous adventure every day."
>
> \- Serge Kahili King

The key factor here is the development of the ability to perform what some see as miracles. In the humblest sense, the Kupua develops these special transformational powers and abilities in order to help others. There are limitless possibilities in unfolding the empowering mana when you accept the kokua mission, which translates as extending loving, sacrificial help to others for their benefit without personal gain. When spiritual power is invoked and carried, it becomes transformational and moves consciousness naturally. Herein lies the *secret* of empowerment. The message of the modern shaman inspires the seekers who are in touch with the ancient masters to unfold the skills and abilities through personal connection to God or a master guide in Spirit.

The modern Kupua doesn't necessarily follow the old Hawaiian religion as practiced by the ancients. Because it involves individual spiritual development, there is no required religious dogma. However, there are principles and universal laws that must be strictly followed. The mystical beliefs and practices are intrinsically linked in consciousness and levels of reality to every phase of esoteric wisdom teachings if one is to truly use the metaphysical aspects and disciplines of Hawaiian mysticism. As the practice of mysticism unfolds in higher consciousness, the ancient knowledge becomes revitalized in your present consciousness. Mystical concepts can certainly be rendered and understood in any language, culture, and in every walk of life. The principles are practical when added to existing systems of belief. Through mystical expansion, a new model of Ho'omana emerges throughout the world.

Mysticism and the Psychic Sense

Psychic and mystical abilities are natural to everyone, which are unfolded, to a greater extent, because of desire, discipline, and direction through service. In some people, intuitive qualities are latent, unrecognized and tucked away unused, waiting to spring into action when called upon. The Hawaiian term to express intuition is *Ike Papalua*. It means, twice seeing. This refers to a development of a refined psychic awareness, which is a valued healing tool. A person initiated with this power didn't necessarily use predictive tools or omens; they just knew (a result of expanded consciousness). Hawaiians expressed this in the *E homai ka'kie Papalua* chant, which means *give us the foresight*.

Ike Papalua means more than just foresight. It is the ability to express intuition as truth, revelation, and insight. It conveys the ability to see beyond the visual world, see beyond the horizon and go deeply inside where truth lives, to know yourself and see far into the past, present and future to explore understanding. In intuitive thinking, the conclusion is immediately known without being aware of its origin. The conscious mind may not be aware of it, but cooperates in its transmittal. To intuit something is to affect the most direct and immediate connection between the subject and its object. Intuitive awareness is a by-product of consciousness expansion. Combined with discipline, selected study in Hawaiian shamanism, and Kupua rituals, intuition naturally develops as the need arises.

> "My ancestors had that ability; I think we all have a bit of it. We just don't exercise it."
>
> - Sabra Kauka
> *Religions, Mythology, and Ritual* (61)

In modern advancing spirituality, every person has the ability to tap into metaphysical empowerment where intuition flourishes. In some, the qualities are latent, unrecognized and tucked away, unused, waiting to be unfolded. Most people use intuition without recognizing the depth of their own abilities. When called upon, they will deny they even have psychic ability, while uttering a profound statement, which clearly is from their inner resources or a Spirit revelation. Psychicism is an ever-evolving skill; the more you use it, the more you have confidence in yourself. When you trust that your intuition brings truth, not only will your psychic sense increase, but also your natural mysticism flow unfolds through your higher Self, which resides within your inner consciousness. In an article published October 13, 1870, *Ka Po'e Kahiko – The People of Old* (54), Samuel Kamakau verified the importance placed upon prophetic utterances:

> "In the old days in Hawaii, prophetic utterances and hidden sayings ('*olelo huna*, i.e., speech with secret meaning) were relied on."

Those who prophesized future events were known as the *Kaula* in whom was manifested the Divine spirit of the great Gods of Hawaii. According to *The Honolulu Advertiser* (1955),

> "The last member of the Council of Prophets, the Kaula, was the great Priest Kapihe, who lived and practiced his skill during the lifetime of Kamehameha. Today another descendant of this great Kapilae still carries on the priestly duties of the Order of the Kaula. He is the widely known David Bray Sr. of Honolulu.

Chapter 3. Ancient Hawaiian Mysteries

To understand the Hawaiian mysteries, we refer to the heritage from which the people originated. Ancient peoples knew of their ancestral connection to the Pleiades, Sirius (the Dog star) and other stars. The star clusters are much revered in the Hawaiian tradition as the place from which they came. Other cultures concur that we are all descendants from the stars. Coming from this common ancestry, we are all one global family rooted in the most ancient traditions. In *Kahuna Source*, Ki'a'i Ho'okahi Weber expressed this cosmic mystery:

> "...High above and far below, in-between and all around, as far out into the vast spark of our electrons. That we are! From the known to the unknown, from the unknown to the known. That we are!"

Sacred Mysteries of Mu

Hawaiian traditions are derived from the ancient motherland called Mu. *The Sacred Symbols of Mu* by Col. James Churchward relates physical evidence of the history of Mu, later called Lemuria. The mysteries were entrusted to the trained masters called Naacals who enlightened the world through the advanced teachings that humans were created in full and perfect form. They also taught there were two forces: the material authority, which emanates from the earthly body and the spiritual influence radiating from the soul. They believed spiritual influences had the power to overcome the material and it was their destiny for the spiritual to eventually dominate.

The secret teachings appear in the mysteries of every religion carrying this hope for humanity. As time goes by, these ancient threads are woven to uplift and point an enlightened way to living the path of aloha and pono heritage.

> "In Lemuria the teachings were pure, balanced, and honored God/Goddess... The ancient mother goddess of Lemuria was known as the beloved goddess Uli. She was the most important deity in the ancient Hawaiian pantheon for she was mother of all the gods and goddesses. Uli is our Spiritual Heavenly Mother, the mother of us all, and the female force of creation... Uli is birther of self, and by her example of self-creation she shows and empowers us in how to create ourselves exactly as we desire. She is the female generative force of the sun, or the Light of Life of the sun - *Ka Wahine Ke La*!"
>
> — Laura Kealoha Yardley, Ph.D.

Hawaiian Theosophy – Ho'omana Kahiko

> "At the dawning, into an amorphous world, were born the founding Gods of tradition whose names were called Kane, Ku, and Lono. Born they were of the sacred breath of I'O, who was, who is, who shall be for time without end. *Eli Eli Tau mai!* Let His Great Peace descend!"

This quotation from the primordial Master Kahiko, identifies the Kumu or source of the Ho'omana Kahiko Theosophy from which Hawaiian theosophical and philosophical tributaries flow. Their mana continues to flow with currents of powerful calm. Theosophy according to Webster implies:

> "...Knowledge of Divine things, i.e. any of various philosophies or religious systems that propose to establish direct contact with Divine principle through

contemplation, revelation, etc. and to gain thereby a spiritual insight superior to empirical knowledge."

Hawaiian Theosophy – Ho'omana Kahiko is ancient *ike* (Divine knowledge). It is the ageless wisdom of empowerment, which is transmitted through Hawaiian spirituality and its traditions. It contains the knowledge of the laws, principles, processes and mysteries of Nature herself in all forms, both objective and subjective. It incorporates all levels of being and operation, physical, emotional, mental, super mental and spiritual mysteries. It aids each person in building a firm spiritual, social and moral compass.

Kahu Brandt taught that the origin of Ho'omana Kahiko is found in the Sacred Triumvirate, the source of all that is. As a Hawaiian theosophist, he described himself as a polytheistic idealist as he worshiped before the altars of the Supreme Triad, hailing them by their beautiful esoteric title, Hika-Po-Loa. He held the proud banner of idealism and emphasized that Hawaiians are transcendentalist, who seek their peace beyond the material universe and strive for perfection in reality through Divine Illumination. Today's contemporary interpretation of ancient theosophy assists in coping with life's complexity.

> "The spiritual side of Ho'omana Kahiko evidences itself by building faith in life, by helping us to discern the meaning of humankind's existence. It aids us in developing a superior intellect plus a certain humility and a real concern for the welfare of our fellow humans, without these qualities, the fullness of life may never be recognized. Ho'omana Kahiko offers the sincere practitioner the very practical surety that he or she is no longer at the mercy of an impersonal, and often callous fate; of knowing that his or her destiny is controllable, and alterable."
>
> - Kahu Lanakila Brandt
> *The Sacred Keys of the Masters, Ho'omana Kahiko* (19)

Po'ohuna – Hawaiian Divine Mysteries

Po'ohuna means to discover the power and authority of ancient Hawaiian Divine mysteries. Kahu Lanakila also referred to po'ohuna as ancient Hawaiian metaphysics. Po'ohuna is discussed from the viewpoints of the Spirit world, the material world, and from the perspective of the practical metaphysical application of the ancient Divine mysteries. We connect to the sacred beginning of humanity and understand that the story of creation is more than the capability of the biological birthing of humans. It is also the metaphysical origin of implanting the Divine Master within, which instills Ho'okumu. Ho'okumu means to create empowerment from within the inner higher consciousness faculties. It is the thrusting forward of something from its source to teach or enlighten another. The energy of the Kumu (master within) is seeded within everyone. This establishes a natural ability to manifest all things directly from source.

The priesthood taught the knowledge of human destiny and transmitted the appropriate levels of consciousness through the carefully orchestrated rituals. In ancient times the people used the sacred names of God to activate the principles and basic patterns by which all energy manifests in form. The language is deliberately expressed in the technical spiritual science of Hawaii. A deeper examination reveals the multi-layered knowledge. However, today, some of the mystery is lost in the transmission of the language consciousness itself. Hawaiian spiritual leader Nana Veary explains:

> "This use of language vanished long ago. Hawaiians today speak the missionary language, a literal type of Hawaiian. The riddle is gone. This is tragic, for when you lose the language, you lose your identity... In order to regain the mystery, we compensate the lack of transmission by delving into the beliefs and practices of the priesthood and of Hawaiian theosophy."

Po - Understanding the World of Spirit

Po is the World of Spirit. It symbolizes the potential of all and at the same time, nothing. It is from nothingness that all is formed. The circle represents the concept of the infinite, eternity, timelessness, the universe, Divine origin, and the spiritual realm of the celestial world. Pertaining to divinity, darkness of the night and other terms, the meaning ranges from the concept of heaven to hell, and much more. When the word Po is used in a phrase, its meaning is revealed by the context within the sentence.

Everyone is eternal in Po. It is both the past and future to the present generation. It is the ultimate origin of all life and life's ultimate destination. Many native Hawaiians use the phrase, *mai ka po mai* (from the night, or since time immemorial) to indicate divinity, wisdom, and traditions that originate in antiquity. The mysterious and infinite ancient Hawaiian Po is the ultimate Kumu (Source) of all Hawaiian gods. Relating to the Halau energy, Po contains many generations of ancestors that brought this generation, as well as future generations, into existence that support and empower you (read *Hawaiian Mythology*). Exploration of Po opens many facets of Divine mysteries. In investigating beliefs about Po, you will find fearful heroes, angry victims, and sad, ravenous spirits. Through the Po, you can enter Milu (the world of the dead, the land of shadows) where you can find, reclaim, and redeem your lost ancestors and other deities. Thus, the concept of Po opens your view of the world of spirit as the source of humanity's beginning and invites you to explore the deeper mysteries in the foundation upon which spiritual and material realities are formulated.

The Kumulipo

Hawaiian mysticism takes you into the interpretations of the Kumulipo and explores a deep awareness of creation and of life. The *Kumu li po* can be translated as the basis of our existence beginning in darkness or source of life, *Po* and weaves an account of the creation of the universe that parallels modern scientific explanations. The research of Clorice B. Taylor (1957) and Lanakila Brandt (1976) depicts a drawing of the 17 abodes for Spirit and humans to occupy. This is the story of the past and future that teaches the evolution of light and life in the present moment. It is viewed from the perspective of the living earth coming from the darkness on which the ancestors' spirits could take form. The Kumulipo teaches us that there is a natural relationship among all living things. We are born into the same earth family as the land, the sea, and the other living creatures. To learn the sacred Hawaiian Kumulipo (creation story) is to understand that the people on earth were molded from the essence (consciousness) of the Supreme Oneness, and this is what is carried in the genes of civilization today.

Within the body of humanity intrinsically breathes the sacred mana, which is accessible to all. When you realize that you are Supreme Essence you can utilize a vast amount of mana. To gain use of your mana, you must accept the individual mastery empowered within you. It is a reference to your own creation in the present moment. The creation story is happening within your own self. You recreate and rebirth yourself every moment. It is an initiation as you awaken to the deeper truths, which lie within your own ancient self. Kahu Brandt explains:

> "When you hear the teaching, 'You were born with the mana of love created.' It is speaking about you, yourself right now, as: Created was the Primary Temple of the Gods... Man."

I'O – Divine Source

I'O (ee-oh) is omniscient, or *all seeing*. "The Supreme God who is with form and without form, who is Eternal Perfection" Popularly called Oi-E (oh ee ay), Supreme One; the I Am Presence.

The circle depicts a person and the point (I'O) is incarnated within. The circle also symbolizes eternity, completion, and perfection with I'O at the center. Other names for I'O (ee-oh) are: Teava, Keawe, IAO, Kela, and Tera. I'O is Infinite Potential, Infinite Source. Aunty Laura Yardley, taught:

> "To the Hawaiian, IAO (or I'O) represents the spirit, the void, ether, the Light. It is the mysterious source from which everything manifests. In other traditions, it is known as the akasha. IAO is timeless and spaceless: it is beyond the beyond."

"I" (ee) means supreme, "O" means being. I'O is usually referred to as Supreme Essence and is the pure Spirit of the Force of Creation. Our existence as a conscious entity is sustained by an energy system, which includes the aura and inner core (I'O). Take yourself into the I'O. It is the Source where there is only pure potential of all Creation. I'O beckons to be viewed and felt in the deepest and most ancient of context; to be sensed as intimate; yet, viewed always open with unrestrictive, new perceptions. Kumukahi is a Hawaiian word, which means "one source," or "source of origin." Other terms that can be used to describe the Omnipresence is the Divine, One Consciousness, God, etc. Expressions to describe Source are *"I"* and *"Akua."* Akua is the most commonly used term for God. Kahuna Harry Jim says,

> "To Hawaiians, God is a verb, an action – not a noun or a name. Emotions too, are actions. God's motive for creation was so that we can experience life more fully and get to know ourselves better. God was motivated to create so that we might find and achieve the ultimate expression of emotional maturity."

IAO - Principle of Divine Energy

IAO is the principle of Divine Energy, which must be learned before any initiate can step into the shaman shoes. These are secret teachings of empowerment published by Kahu David Bray and Douglas Low in *The Kahuna Religion of Hawaii* (29-30):

Everything is a manifestation of Divine Energy. Divine Energy is neither self-existent nor self-created, but depends upon the mysterious source symbolized by Ancient Hawaiians in the name I-A-O. In order to have the right to verbalize the sacred name in olden times, you had to first seek to find the meaning held within I-A-O. The outline of developing access is:

I (Ee): denotes the Supreme as in the creative act by which that which is perfect manifests the creator who is perfect and can only create that which is perfect. It is necessary to get to know the energies and principles of "I," the Supreme.

A (Ah): indicates the radiating of Divine Energy in the multidimensional universe, which shows humans how to be healthy, live happily and advance spiritually. Demonstrate "A."

O (Oh): means developing the ability of being; to make reality of Divine power; and experience unreality as well. "O" functions in the Divine Energy of being. You must be able to manifest through this essence for yourself and others.

IAO (Ee Ah Oh): You must first learn the individual principles of **I**: Divine Energy Creative Act, **A**: Radiate in multidimensional universes, and **O**: Develop the ability to make Reality of Divine power. When you are able to live and manifest it for yourself and others, you are ready to speak and activate the principles.

The IAO Process

Ancient Hawaiians expressed the belief and worship of one God comprised of three equal Beings. The Beings were worshiped as one under the mysteries of Hika-Po-Loa, Oi-e signifying *Most Excellent, Supreme*, and *Ku-kauhai*, meaning the *One Established*. Some believe these names were probably titles of the One true God - the true name being I'O. Aunty Laura's teaching include the IAO Process and Principles from Daddy Bray:

> "All manifestations function in terms of polarity and periodicity. Polarity divides the one energy into a dynamic dualism of interaction. Periodicity arranges the modes of interaction into an orderly hierarchy. The IAO is the

unmanifested point through which manifestation and creation occur."

Using this linear framework, all matter is manifested as a duality in the density of human interaction. IAO, being pure Spirit, is the energy the Kupua uses to manifest in the higher consciousness strength. This is how the transformative process works:

IAO The IAO point (dot) represents Spirit, Etheric, and the Light. IAO is the point where all manifestation and
• creation occurs. Spirit (IAO) is unmanifested energy.

Matter is manifested in the density of the physical world as duality and separateness expertise.

IAO in the Material

Duality is density (the line). Density individualizes the oneness of IAO (dots). IAO is the unrealized potential ready to create reality. IAO will assist to create on either polarity chosen. There is constant struggle to push the boundaries of limitations imposed by the lower consciousness density and duality beliefs.

Triangulation

Triangulation transcends duality and creates a third part. It is the key to complete duality in the spiritual and material aspects of incarnation. A significant shift occurs when we integrate the internal spirituality and the duality of the external world. Through melding the sacred and profane, we are challenged to transform opposition into paradox. During this period, we are driven to label all sides of an issue (or pairs of opposites) to exist in equal meaning until our hidden unity is revealed. The process of triangulation demands a change in beliefs. It allows us to prepare to move past the duality into functioning in the higher consciousness Oneness. Once the lessons (illusions) of duality are learned, transcendence of density is anchored through integration of the IAO process. This combines Aloha and Mana, resulting in Pono (perfect) manifestation.

Higher Consciousness Oneness

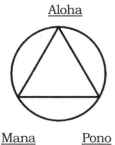

Aloha

Mana   Pono

The IAO process facilitates rising above the density to the higher levels of consciousness in which the density ceases to exist to attain the desired transcendence. Triangulation of the qualities of Aloha, Mana and Pono signifies the unifying Lokahi of the three selves.

Unity (Lokahi) of the Three Selves

The symbol of the fully integrated (Spirit, Mind, Body) human is accomplished through the unity of the three selves in higher truth (Lokahi). The individual literally moves from duality into higher levels of oneness, thereby transcending the density (base nature), which created the duality in the first place.

This encircled illustration depicts completion of the process with IAO firmly residing within the center as an indication that a transformation has taken place. Lokahi is the inherent unity of the selves that join the spiritual and material world in a cohesive harmony and balance.

Uli – Sacred Mother of Creation – Daughter of I'O

Uli is described as the spiritual heavenly mother, the sacred mother of creation and the daughter of I'O. She was recognized as the most important female deity in the ancient Hawaiian pantheon of gods, for she was the mother of gods and goddesses and the tutelary deity of the entire body. It was Uli who released the Living Water that flowed in the Breath of Life from Keawe to the females of earth. Uli is called the "Birther of Self." It is by her example of self-creation that we are inspired to create ourselves in the image we most desire.

> "And he breathed once more and gave Life to the celestial sister-bride of Kane, called *Uli-la'a-a-Kane*, Uli-sacred-to-Kane and worshiped as *Wahine-a-ka-La'a-a-Kea*, or Woman-of-the-Sacred-Light and *Uli-a-ke-ouli-lani*, Uli-of-the-omen-bearing-heavens. It is she who is Guardian or aumakua of the Hawaiian priesthood, *Ke Oihana Kahuna.*"

The ancients referred to Uli as the goddess with the discerning eye who perceived everything that transpired on Earth. Sometimes the Kahuna spoke of her as *Uli Nana Hew*, meaning Uli sees all injustice and unrighteousness. Other times the goddess was spoken of as *Uli Nana Pono*, meaning Uli beholds all justice and righteousness. Laura Kealoha Yardley teaches:

> "The Kahunas of Hawaii were guardians of this ancient lineage of the great Goddess Uli, as well as caretakers of the esoteric knowledge. For a long time, the carefully guarded secrets were in the hands of only the most high priests and seers, and the knowledge of Uli gradually went underground and the balance was upset. Now, however, the energy of Uli is available to all who call upon her. She is again coming forth to facilitate the remembering of this ancient wisdom, and to bestow her blessings on all those who turn to her."

The Pantheon

An introduction to the pantheon is given to understand the Hawaiian view of the universe as a monad and its hierarchy that serves the individual. The general structure outlines the many conceptual forms of the Supreme God-Source. Contained within it are the spirit forces of creation (I'O), which define the consciousness flowing from the I'O, (Omnipresence, the I Am Presence) and Kumukahi (source of origin) into the physical space of our universe. It is in this belief system of the spiritual and material world that we can know and connect with God and in some manner understand our own existence. The energy of the Pantheon identified as I'O (Universal Mind) encompasses all spirits that serve to benefit the mission of all that is within the realm of earth. The core, viewed in universal terms, is incarnated within every individual as the Divine Spark of God. The complete Hawaiian cosmology occupies an entire chapter of the theosophical text written by Kahu Lanakila as a means to preserve its cultural and theosophical value.

> "There is a natural and harmonious order to the entire universe. The three major forces are the gods and goddesses, nature, and man. The Hawaiian of old realized that it was necessary that these forces be kept in "harmony" and that they were all in some way interrelated."
>
> - Aunty Laura Kealoha Yardley
> *Heart of Huna*

The Spiritual Hierarchy

The ancient Hawaiians came to know the monad intimately in their sacred multiplicities through the hierarchy of the Four, Four Hundred, Four Thousand, Forty Thousand, and Four Hundred Thousand Beings who were birthed as servitors from the individualized God image of Kane (Ka'i-i'mamao). They are All and They are Three. The main classifications of the pantheon are:

- Hika-Po-Loa: Kane, Ku, and Lono
- Akua: Four supreme gods: Kane, Ku, Lono, Kanaloa
- Kupua: god-goddess linked to a certain expertise, guardian spirits: aumakua, personal and family gods

The Hika-Po-Loa is an embodiment of the I'O as a God-head that establishes a powerful mana connection with humanity. The sacred dimensions are expressed as three individual deities and as one. The second division of the hierarchy begins the almost limitless functional personification of Hika-Po-Loa in the Four Hundred, most of whose titles begin with the key name of the Source and end with a functional identification. The lesser god-goddess and spirits naturally have far-reaching and multiple identities in order to help humanity in their mission.

Everything is God and everything is an incarnation of the higher energies. God is expressed as clouds, rain, movement of lava, earth, currents of ocean and of air to name just a few. All things seen and unseen are God-expressed and therefore are expressed as god–goddess or Spirit.

In the third level are *Na Puali Alii Akua*, the Godly Host. This Kupua assembly is composed of Aumakua and Kumupa'a, High Spirit Guardians or Family Guardians, one synonymous with the other. This group includes well-known Hula Goddess Laka and a few Kane, Ku, and Lono personifications who serve in dual roles at both master and median levels. Most notable are Ku-ka-ili-moku, war god of the conqueror Kamehameha who united the islands and Pele with her eight sisters and five brothers. The Kupua akua include those who demonstrate magic, have super powers, and can assume various body forms called kinolau, e.g. Pele, Mo'o or Giant Lizard gods, and Pueo (Owl) gods.

The worship of family aumakua, or ancestral figures, link the current generation to generations past, connecting to the very origins of the world. Information about family aumakua can be very personal. Therefore, it is shared only with family members. An aumakua is a relative, so the connection between the family and gods is compassionate and reciprocal. Aumakua can speak directly and also appear as signs or omens to convey meaning for the family. Every family had ancestors who became deified and transfigured over time as gods or emerged from eternity (Po). Mary Kawena Pukui could recall the names of fifty known aumakua in her own family. According to Pukui, aumakua bring a warning of coming misfortune or provide deliverance from immediate dangers. They also warn or reprimand during dreams and visions.

The stories of Hawaiian gods and aumakua contain infinite variety but all reflect the core values of their society. Today, as in ancient times, individuals can follow the spiritual path of the ancestors to turn to the gods and goddesses for relief from their physical, emotional, mental, and spiritual problems. The people gain mana (Divine power) through ancient rites and discover the solutions through prayer, meditation, and other spiritual practices of the ancient pantheon consciousness.

Chapter 4. Spirits of Humanity

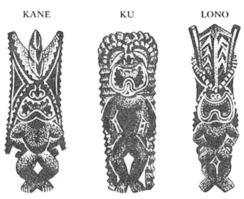

Hika-Po-Loa - Triumvirate: Kane, Ku, and Lono

The founding Gods of tradition comprise the God-head, which was born from the sacred breath of I'O. The Hika-Po-Loa - Triumvirate is worshiped as One Triune Source who is revered independently as the beloved empowering gods Kane, Ku, and Lono. The individual divinities are known through stories and legends. People related to how the gods completed the tasks in life the same way a human would cope with life as they walked, talked and worked with them. In Polynesia, the three primary emanations of the Source form the highest Trinity. The spiritual dimensions of Hika-Po-Loa are linked to the people through an intimate relationship and connection through daily bonding. The people faithfully attuned with their God-consciousness and dedicated themselves to using God-mana to live a life of pono.

Divine Triad Mo'olelo

The Divine Triad mo'olelo as taught by Kahu Brandt describes the creation of this world. Kahu depicted the birthing of Hika-Po-Loa, the Divine Triad:

> "...Boundless night lying in total silence over endlessly churning stygian waters. By even then, Life existed, one Supreme Intelligence... *'Ke Kumu'* - the Root, the Core... of all that is, ever shall be, a fiery mist beyond the pale, I'O. ...the world knew <u>Light</u>, <u>Stability</u>, and <u>Sound</u>. The Sacred Triad was born, born of the HA. The sacred breath of I'O, equal in nature but disparate in Their gifts, equal in Their Divinity but distinct in Their attributes."

The Divine Triad

Kane: *Nui-Akea* or *Kiekie-Loa*, Creator and Supreme Intelligence. First Born, of I'O, considered the superior of the other two, is called by the sacred titles, *Ka'i-i mamao*, The Supreme and *Kane-Kumu-Honua*, Kane the Creator of the Earth. Kane is worshiped as *Kane-Nui-Akea*, God of Light.

Ku: *Ka Pao* (strong). Second Born, Ku is the Builder and Architect of the material world. He is the God of Stability and worshiped as *Ku-Nui-Akea*.

Lono: – *Noho-I-Ka-Wai*, Dwelling on the Water rose from the face of the waters, the world-encompassing tides of *Kai Pele*, the rolling volcanic sea. The God of Sound, he was called *Lono-Nioho-I-Ka-Wai, Lono-Puha*, Lono who destroys illness.

In the rites of the temple, they are worshiped jointly as Hika-Po-Loa and they are also worshiped individually under their sacred names: Kane-nu-akea, Ku-nui-akea and Lono-nui-akea, as times and circumstances indicated. The Trinity-worship of the adoration of Light, Stability and Sound was conducted with solemn ritual and embodied in the magnificent hymns in the ancient Hawaiian Island and the Marquesas.

Created from eternity, Hika-Po-Loa Triumvirate Godhead group, Kane, Ku, and Lono or the Triune-God aspect operates within the realm of Earth. In Earth incarnations, the same system of creation described of the gods is replicated in humans and also describes the formula for creation and functioning of all things. Thus, follows the Hawaiian belief, "as it is above, so it is below."

The Hika-Po-Loa created *Kanaka* (people) molded from the sacred red earth (*ala-ea*) and whitish palolo clay. They blended their own *wai-nao* (saliva) and breathed their own sacred mana. Thus, people are able to have two separate souls or spirits, considered to be their conscious and subconscious minds (*Uhane* and *Unihipili*). These are joined with a third higher consciousness (Aumakua). Dr. Laura Yardley references this relationship in *The Heart of Huna* (44):

> "In addition to these two parts of man, there is a third that the Kahuna called Aumakua (Higher Self, God Self). Sometimes called 'superconscious'... All three selves play their distinct and quite a unique role in the life of each of us. The important thing is that they are working in harmony and cooperate with one another."

Unihipili, Uhane, and Aumakua

The Triune Spirits of human life are the composite power, the Mauli (Triad). It is our sacred life principle (spiritual virtue), our effectiveness and consciousness. Individually, each represent minds, separate and distinct from the other, that must be in harmony and balance to work together as one cohesive unit.

> "The Three aspects of Selves are the three spirits of humanity, which are called *Unihipili*, *Uhane*, and *Aumakua* as identified by Hawaiian theosophy used to enrich your life."
>   - Kahu Lanakila Brandt

Unihipili – Ku: The Unihipili is the spiritual foundation upon which things can be established in the physical world. In the inner aspect, it is the Subconscious Mind (body soul) of a person. Physically, it is literally the bones of a person, which are buried (the physical essence of a person where the mana of the memory is stored). Unihipili is the Subconscious Mind, which most of us do not know. It uses gut feelings (intuition) to be known; it is highly ethical, discriminates good from bad, right from wrong and discerns aloha/pono expressions.

Ku (not capitalized) means here or present. The Subconscious Mind (ku) knows. The responsibility (*kuleana*) encompasses all physical and mechanical movements and actions of the body. In the unconscious characteristics, ku supplies emotional energy and memory. The god Ku (capitalized) influence is the energy of the rising sun and prayers are directed to the east, where the sun rises. In modern teaching, God Ku supports the Unihipili.

Uhane – Lono: Uhane is the reasoning Spirit, which resides in the brain-body. It does not independently move the body although it is the motivating force. Uhane is the investigatory Spirit of humanity that travels and observes in the etheric. In the inner aspects, Uhane is the Conscious Mind called the Conscious Self (intellect) known as the mental soul. It is the logical, reasonable, rational part of you that you know. It is the thinker, analyzer, director, and decision-maker.

Lono (not capitalized) identifies the intellect of the Conscious Self and has control of the Thinking Mind. It has the power to decide, and in this activity calls on the god Lono for assistance. Lono is the god of yielding power, called the Lord of Peace, who is the harvest god of agriculture and healing depicted as rainfall that nurtures and restores. Lono appears in the wet season as rain clouds and winter storms. Appearance of the star cluster Makali'i (Pleiades) signals the Makahiki season celebration of Lono. Lono strengthens the intellectual mission of the Uhane.

Aumakua – Kane: Aumakua (capitalized) is the God Self and means parent, guardian or guide. It never resides in the body, as do Uhane and Unihipili Spirits. Aumakua: Personal, ancestral, and immortal spiritual aspect or oversoul; Higher Self, God Self,

Angelic, and Spiritual Self from which we are sourced into life and into which all our former lives are archived. It is the Parental Spirit, which is always with you and is as near as a call of prayer, with a spiritual power supply for you to utilize. Understanding the levels of higher consciousness of the role of the Aumakua include the highest Spirit, guardian angel as well as ancestral aumakua and helpers. He or she is your ready protector and trustworthy guiding Spirit through life and by extension, the guide and protector of your immediate family. Your personal guiding force is the Spirit part of you, which you feel as your spiritual nature that yearns to know God.

Kane is representative of the Aumakua; he is the main god of creation, the forces of nature, the giver of life and sustains human life. This is depicted as the one who provides fresh water (mana) and along with Kanaloa they are the main creators of water sources. Kane is the sunlight and water combined. The rainbow, lightning, and thunder are all sacred signs that Kane is present to work together.

Akua - The Four Gods

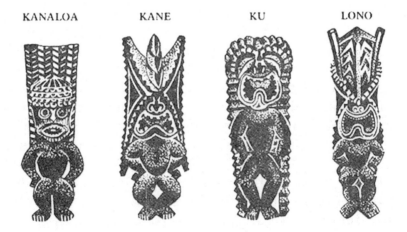

The images represent the beloved and revered Hawaiian gods (*Akua*), the awesome power they shared with humanity and depict a time when the gods walked the earth as men. These Tiki were made for the tourist market; originally, an uncarved upright stone represented Kane. The later carvings provided standardized statues on which to meditate. These Tiki images remind us how close the realms of the gods were to the people. It humanizes the layers of consciousness (gods) and in a tangible way, prove that gods truly exist in a form that humans can relate to in the unseen and in the physical world. The people emulated the principles and values of the gods in their worship and in their daily life. In Maori mythology, the Tiki represents the first man created and symbolizes deified ancestors. According to history, Hawaiians are descended from the lineage of the gods. The Tiki connects people to the idea that God actually is expressed in physical form today as it was for the ancestors. These images re-enforce that this oneness relationship is even now available for them.

Akua relates to the four gods Kane, Ku, Lono, and Kanaloa. These four are worshiped as Kane, the god of sky and creation; Ku, the god of war and prosperity, awareness (contemplation) and many forms of artisanry; Lono, the god of peace, rain, and fertility; and Kanaloa, the god of the ocean who brings mana and healing. They are the highest Akua who are intimate gods, spirits, and helpers who not only attend and guide humanity, but also live within them. When we talk about the different gods acknowledged as the triune spirits of humanity and other cherished pantheon members, we are talking about intimate relationships. This paints the portrait of personal relationships not only between the Divine and humans, but also depicts the intimacy between all things. The gods exemplified important principles and values to the people. The four major gods all had orders of priesthood in which to teach, maintain connection with the people, and assist them to evolve spiritually and materially. The primary influence in human consciousness is:

1. Kane/Aumakua (the High Self or God Self) is where the Triune God and the spirits are always attending the Soul. Kane represents awakening consciousness.

2. Ku/Unihipili (Lower Self), animal nature, where the subconscious (unconscious) mind thread of awareness and emotions reside in the body memory of evolution.

3. Lono/Uhane (Middle Self) is the conscious mind will power to choose from the information it discovers.

a. The lower and middle selves work closely together

4. Kanaloa (Core Self) is how human mana flows. This is the concept God and I are One:
    a. Integrates and binds all things in the spiritual power (mana) humans use to live their lives

This is a recap to view the inner Spirit and major gods with their relationship to the Triune Person and their three selves:

Inner Spirit	Major God	Triune Person Relationship
Hika-Po-Loa	Trinity	Mind, Body and Spirit/Triad Power
Aumakua	Kane	Personal God/Higher Self
Unihipili	Ku	Physical Spirit/Subconscious Self
Uhane	Lono	Reasoning Spirit/Conscious Self
I'O	Kanaloa	Material/Spiritual integration, Core Self

The Kanaloa Connection

KANALOA

Kanaloa serves humanity as one of the four akua (gods) facilitating the flow of mana. A root meaning of ka na loa is the great peace or the great stillness. In the esoteric Kupua tradition, Kanaloa is known as a god of healing and lord of the ocean (a symbol of mana). The ocean is thought to be one of his bodies, as are many sea creatures like the shark, octopus, and squid. The word for octopus/squid is *he'e*, meaning to flow as in the flowing of the life force that causes sickness to flee away. Other ocean-related kinolau (bodies) are the *nai'a* (dolphins) and the *kohola* (whales).

Kanaloa stands as an integrated god-human figure (Spirit in matter), living in the physical world. His Tiki presents a being with eyes wide open with complete awareness of the spiritual and physical world. The carved high headdress shows the knowledge of Divine conscious connection (mana, the power of creative thought). The streamers descending past his shoulders depict his direct involvement with the physical world. He represents the Core Self or the center of the Universe (I'O) that is flowing within you. The ancient legends described Kanaloa as the brother and traveling companion of Kane, the god of creation. Accepted on equal terms, the gods physically walked and worked together on earth to complete co-creative tasks. The Kanaloa connection is the model of the Triune Person who is also called the Triune Self.

The Triune Person

What you may think of yourself, as a singular Self, is actually a composite, a matrix, and a personal soul cluster. You are composed of a functionally distinct soul, as well as a fullness of Spirit (all aspects of God). In human terms, the Triune Self refers to your Self as being a multiplicity of God spirits (the Sacred Triumvirate). In fact, you have all aspects of God living within you. Kahuna Harry Uhane Jim explains this relationship in his book *Wise Secrets of Aloha:*

> "Here's how the Hawaiian kahunas understood the complex physical psyche of a human being. They use three terms – *Au'makua, Uhane, and Unihipili* – for the triune human being. Greet these important words and bring their essence into your awareness. Breathe them in. They are the triune self, who you really are.
> Once you have mastered these Hawaiian terms you can better understand the methodology of Lomilomi. For Lomilomi shifts the energies locked in the body by unlocking the triune aspects into flow."

The three gods together describe the whole person (the integration of God into yourself to live as one). One factor is that you have the ability to use mana for practical purpose in the pragmatic physical world. Hawaiian theosophy clarifies how physically incarnated humans interact with Spirit, and how the Spirit world is available in every aspect to help humanity. Whatever happens on any level of reality (physical, emotional, mental or spiritual) also happens on every other level. The teaching relates to the profound metaphysical truth that humanity was created in the image of the same triplicity ascribed to God. Brad Steiger, internationally known psychic researcher in *Kahuna Magic* says:

> "...Man may come to see himself in a clearer light. We may trade simplicity for the triplicity of being, he admits, but orthodox Christianity has accustomed us to consider God a triplicity. Apparently, we have lost sight of man as a similar triplicity."

The Sacred Triumvirate is a coalition of three Divine energies that form an alliance to support humanity. In *The Sacred Keys of the Master* (25, 26), Kahu Lanakila explains the Sacred Triumvirate in relation to the human pathway through life:

> "Our bodies are the primary temples of the Hika-Po-Loa, The Sacred Triumvirate, from whom all mana flows and as such possess many amazing powers and capabilities, which require only mana to turn them into super powers."

The Six Empowerments of the Body Temple

Your physical body is a temple comprised of seven bodies. The first three recognized by Western science are solids, liquids, and gases. The four known by mystics are *Mahele Kino Aka* (ethers). It is a sacred place where your soul resides that is the mold or pattern upon which your dense physical form is constructed. Your human temple is designed to reflect the perfect unity of the body, mind, and soul trinity. It is a partnership involving awareness, direct communication, and equal cooperation. The body-temple must be kept holy in order to generate mana and maintain its flow. Kahu Lanakila said that abusing your temple drains your powers and brings confusion and chaos to your life. These are the six empowering results when you treat your body as a temple:

1. Life Experience: Present life experiences give power to:
   a. Utilize talents acquired in earlier lives
   b. Discharge past-life obligations
   c. Acquire new talents

2. Attune PEMS Relationship: Attuning the PEMS (physical, emotional, mental, and spiritual) faculties requires lokahi for growth of higher consciousness through these mana-charging processes:
   a. Connect daily via meditation, ESP, mind-travel, power-healing, spiritual-mental-physical disciplines
   b. Mana from one faculty directly affects another

3. Inner Knowledge: Body Temple knowledge imparts the power of wisdom. It combines the most vital elements and translates them into an effective and empowering force to:
   a. Integrate and teach the ancient eternal truths
   b. Interpret for today's enhancement

4. Universal Mana: The higher dimensions of life are peopled by gods, your parental spirits, and powerful nature forces. Their lives and your life are made of the same material. You connect with them to empower yourself to:
   a. Tap into the higher dimensions
   b. Expand your powers from their strength

5. Knowing Your Self: Knowing the inner self is the blissful essence of your own Being. It is your true nature beyond the layers of conditioned identities. To safeguard your sacredness you must:
   a. Keep your temple holy if you want to increase and maintain your power contact
   b. Increase or decrease Mana/power by your choices

6. Personal Control: The power and care of your temple is your responsibility (*kuleana*). The spiritual and material well-being brings rewards and consequences. Spiritual and material matters affect life in these ways:
   a. A spiritually motivated life creates love and pono
   b. A materially motivated life is an unfulfilled search

Chapter 5. The Kahuna

Kahuna is defined in Pukui & Elbert's *Hawaiian Dictionary* as a "priest, sorcerer, magician, wizard, minister, and expert in any profession (whether male or female)." The Kahuna title imparts the mystery of ancient Hawaiian metaphysical teaching. To learn the empowering ways of *Hawaiian Shamanism* and the secrets to empower yourself, seek to know the Kahuna thinking.

> "The way of the real Kahunas of Hawaii was through selfless service, which alone truly allows joy in the beauty of nature to combine with mutual love. Selfless service allows joy in the beauty of nature to combine with mutual love. Such a person is fit to understand and utter the Sacred name of IAO."
>
> - Daddy Bray and David Low

Introduction – The Kahuna

An awakened teacher was known as a Kahuna. They were trusted as a master because they had mastered the subtle and sacred secrets of aloha practice and served the people in the highest measure of integrity. They were known by the power of their presence, which came from living in right relationship with the Divine, in a state of lokahi (inherent unity of oneness), in right relationships with their own heart and with all things. The Kahuna led by becoming the sacred way of Light. In the early days, they gave the teaching to the respected ruling elders, who assimilated the way of Light into their lives. They in turn taught the parents, who accepted living in the wisdom of their higher spiritual consciousness (*mana'o io ao*); the parents taught their children how to live the sacred ways of oneness.

Higher consciousness perpetuated the lineage of the Kahuna teaching in the very intimacy aloha and pono divinely supports. Each person in turn, being in right relationship with the Divine within their own hearts, achieved a state of inherent oneness (*lokahi*) with all things. The higher state of consciousness pervaded. The people lived aloha-love themselves, within their own families and communities and developed a system to ensure alignment with lokahi radiant harmony. They created sacred protocol to establish rules to ensure right relations (pono) as a minimum standard in the community. Each person accepted and perpetuated an extraordinary relationship with the Divine in everything they did. Therefore, everyone cultivated excellence and mastery in their individual field of expertise.

According to the story told by Kaili'ohe Kame'ekua of Kamalo, Moloka'i, recorded in *Tales from the Night Rainbow*, the word Kahuna was not used much because the term was not as revered by them as it later became. It would be placed in front of a title to designate the person was an expert in his or her field when the person excelled above all others. They became the keeper of the secrets. The references here have to do with the mastery of the keepers of the ancient spiritual knowledge with no rank of importance given or implied to the expertise of their work or service being more important than another.

> "Kahu implies the most intimate and confidential relations between the god and its guardian or keeper, while the word Kahuna suggests more of the professional relation of the priest to the community."
>
> - Mary Kawena Puki & Samuel Elbert
> *Hawaiian Dictionary*

The term Shaman is a more modern term. Kahuna is used more frequently in place of master to indicate an empowered person who has attained the highest position in his or her profession. The titles carry the honor and respect earned by the level of their achievement. To many, the designations of Kahu, Kahuna, or Shaman are interchangeable. The modern translation of Kahuna by the Hawaii Cultural and Spiritual Services Center (2017) is:

> "The Hawaiian word *kahuna* translates into English as a priest, minister or expert in any profession; and to act as a priest or expert. Traditionally, the term kahuna generically referred to a learned person who possessed specialized skills and expertise in a professional field of study. In the days of old Hawaii, the kahuna was considered the scholarly equivalent to the academic doctorates of our time. Highly respected as master practitioners of their art or craft, they represented a very powerful elite class within the overall hierarchy of early Hawaiian society. The kahuna was acknowledged as the official keepers of the ancient knowledge and profound wisdom of the early Hawaiians."

Morrnah Nalamaku Simeona, a Native Hawaiian Kahuna honored as a "Living Treasure" and gifted healer, cultivated her family system of healing based on ancient spiritual traditions of ho'oponopono. An inexhaustible educator, Kahu Simeona said:

> "While there is no direct translation for '*Kahuna*,' literally '*Ka*' means light and '*Huna*' means secret, as in sacred wisdom. However, a Kahuna, having the power of a Shaman, the focused training of an expert, and the mystical links of a priest, is a spiritual leader and reverent caretaker of her or his community and ways of Righteousness, the Pono, merging the inner and outer worlds into blended harmony."

Po'okahuna – Priests of Divine Mysteries

The priests who knew Po'okahuna are priests who understood the metaphysical Divine mysteries and are familiar with every phase of Kahuna practices. They had the power to heal through prayer and faith, to prophesy and to interpret omens. Daddy Bray identified himself as Po'oKahuna (Master of metaphysical Divine mysteries) as well as a healing Kahuna called Lapa'au in *The Kahuna Religion of Hawaii* (4). He said that the Kahuna are a class of trained people who serve humanity for goodness and truth. Their goal is to align to the God of Light Within during all life challenges and the demands service to humanity presents. The priest of Divine mysteries was required to know and control the negative forces of his or her own nature. The Kahuna studies about the negative forces in the lowest and highest of all things, which applies to learning from all life experiences. *The Kahuna Religion of Hawaii* (43) explains:

> "Kahunas must master the positive and negative forces. The positive power works through the heavenly, while the negative works through the material. The material and psychical are sometimes called 'earthbound.' This means the forces of the negative work through the psychic and earthly elements. The positive is mental, spiritual, and beyond the normal conditions of human life in its physical and emotional aspects.
>
> It is obvious then, that those polarities must be brought together for completeness. In order to do this, Kahunas have to understand the way energy flows through their own bodies. There is a definite localization of positive and negative poles, a pattern for the flow of energy, and a method of harmonization."

The Hawaiian Kahuna Coded System

The mystical knowledge and ancient wisdom was learned through a special encoded language, which provided a means of giving both a metaphysical and an ordinary meaning to any word or statement. Leinani Melville said that the wise men of ancient Hawaii who composed the original language embedded within the root meanings of words several definitions that often were not remotely connected. The words used in the secret code or vernacular of the priesthood (*Ke oihana kahuna*) often had double, triple, and quadruple meanings. Only the Kahuna mystics and initiates who had been admitted to the inner mystical circle could understand and converse freely with one another in the esoteric meaning. The masters of old were religionists and Hawaiian dialect masters, as was my teacher, Kahu Lanakila Brandt. They were able to convey hidden meaning, mana and the desired consciousness. Much of this deeper Kahuna mystical expertise has been lost with the passing of the masters and the modernization of the Hawaiian language. Interpretation of words and phrases are understood from the information that has been passed on by the Elders. The modern Kahuna mystics glean the esoteric messages and discern the layers of hidden consciousness on a very intuitional level. To gain a mystical understanding, I refer to the *Esoteric Hawaiian Dictionary* by Leinani Melville including the *Esoteric Code of the Hawaiian Kahuna*, as well as Pukui and Elbert's *Hawaiian Dictionary*, and definitions from my teachers, which are not found in any publication. Review the words used in Hawaiian spirituality, which activate the definition in the coded system of multi-layered meaning. Some definitions I use are:

Hawaiian Definitions

A: Ignites and radiates Divine energy, of, connected, related to
Aka: Spiritual essence, reflection of the self, reflection of light
Ala: Path, anointed way, awaken, arise from sleep, stay awake
A'o: Illuminate, fill with the Light; denotes the conscious mind
Alo: Divine breath of life, face-to-face, sharing
Aloha: Be in the presence of the Divinity, deep love
E (Ay): Calling out, term of endearment, spreading mana
Ha: Breath of life, breathe higher consciousness, four
Hana: Work, deed, activity
Ho'o: Cause to happen, expression to make it happen
Hakalau: Meditation, shift into a higher state of awareness
Ho'ohana: Value of worthwhile work
Ho'omana: Cause the mana of the sacred teaching, mystical wisdom, to empower, to worship
Ho'omana Maoli: Most ancient spiritual practices
Honua: Earth, world
Ho'oponopono: Harmony and balance, restore pono
Hu: Forces of movement, chaos, change, spreading outward
Huna: Of the inner world, hidden, invisible, secret knowledge
I (EE): God, I'O, manifesting the perfect, Supreme, best, great
Ike: Spiritual power, knowledge, revelations from the gods
I'O: Supreme Source, Soul of the world, Higher Self, true

IAO: Spirit, Infinite Light, Light of the World, Source
Ka: The, substance, essence of a subject, belong, illumination
Ka Hana Pono: The work of right action, doing what is right
Kahu: Leader, teacher, minister, guardian, keeper, care giver
Kahuna Kupua: Master of Spirits, Mystic, Shaman
Kahuna Kupua A'o: Teacher of enlightenment, self-realization
Ka 'ike huna: Knowledge of the inner world
Kaona: Deeper level, hidden meaning
Kahu na: Expert teacher of inner wisdom, keeper of balance
Ka u: Radiation of light from the heart
Kokua: Loving sacrificial help to others
Kukui: Inner Light in a balanced individual
Kumukahi: God, One source, the Divine, One Consciousness
Kupono: Value of integrity, to move straight toward a goal
Kuu: Let go, as in meditation
La: God, sun, day or light, in distinction from po or darkness
Lau: Vision spreads out, a function in Hakalua trance
Makani: Wind
Maika'i: Excellent, good, good progress
Mana: Life Force, supernatural or Divine power
Mana'o: Empowerment within your mind, beliefs true to you
Na: Plural, calm, forces of stillness, order, form
Na'au: Mind, heart, affections of the heart and mind
Na'au ao: Learned, enlightened, intelligent, wise, knowledge
Nalu: Go inside something, discern, ponder, contemplate
O: Divine Force, Being, directs mana, function in Divine Energy
Ola: Life, good health, well-being, save a life as in healing
Pa'a: Now
Pa hana ko'iko'i: Inner work discipline
Pau: Finished, an ending
Po: Spiritual realm, denotes the subconscious mind
Pono: Rectitude, uprightness and goodness, right action
Po'ohuna: Mysterious, hidden, invisible, as the gods
Po'okahuna: Priests who know the Divine mysteries
U: Seat of emotions, radiation of light from the heart, source
Ulu: Inspire into life, cause to grow, a creator
Ulukau: Intuition, having intuitive abilities

Message From A Hawaiian Kahuna

The personal nature of the Kahuna, and knowledge of God-like qualities stemming from his or her power, philosophy and theosophical beliefs can best be known through an intimate association with and through dedicated study with a Hawaiian master. I honor all who have devoted their lives in such mastery level development and service. Here is a glimpse into the spiritual connection of Po'oKahuna David Kaonohiokala Bray through his thoughts about living the principles and his dedication to the meaning and practice of Aloha as written in *The Kahuna Religion of Hawaii*:

> *"Aloha to the Hawaiian of old is God in us. It means, 'Come forward, be in unity and harmony with your real self, God, and mankind. Be honest, truthful, patient, kind to all forms of life, and be humble.' Kahunas had to learn these things. When they learned them, they found God. They beheld nature as God created it. Beauty in nature is found in flowers, trees, and every living thing on earth, sea, air and fire. Even the rocks and stones and earth have life, according to this way. Kahunas saw beauty, but many of us created ugliness in our hearts and call life sin. Sin is self-made law, not God's law. The kahunas learned from the beginning to be fearless and overcome doubt. Fear causes emotional confusion. Doubt causes emotional confusion. When the mind is confused we say that matter controls mind. Broken homes, loss of friends, and ruin in business result. Fear and doubt create false gods. The forces of darkness surround you and come to dwell in you. Kahunas teach freedom from Satan, whom (Christian) Hawaiians call Milu, by conquering fear and doubt. This booklet tells my story of life as a kahuna. I am one of an old tradition. Many of old were greater than I am. The world is seeking truth, and for this reason I am telling these events. May the Great Power bless you!"*

Teaching - Ho'omana Kahiko and Huna

Ho'omana Kahiko refers to the ancient spiritual knowledge as the Kahuna lived, knew and perpetuated its truth and power. Ho'omana is the foundation of the power and presence of Hawaiian spirituality and the higher consciousness practices.

Huna is a Hawaiian word meaning secret knowledge. Modern teachers use it to describe the overall esoteric teaching of the Kahuna philosophy. The understanding of Huna described here comes from the Kupua tradition and other established Hawaiian teachers, which is the modern or Western accepted term for the esoteric belief system of the Kahuna metaphysical practice.

To learn the empowering ways of Ho'omana Kahiko and the secrets to empower yourself, seek to know the teaching and disciplines of the Kahuna. The knowledge of Kahuna instruction unites the conscious and subconscious minds in order to open to the guidance and blessings of your higher self. The information in this book encompasses the sacred wisdom of Ho'omana Kahiko (ancient practice of empowerment) from the Lono and Kane traditions and links with the practices of the modern Kahuna. The philosophy of modern shamanism called Huna is contemporary esoteric metaphysics adapted from Polynesia that can be understood by individuals living in today's communities. Many shaman live in a bustling community, hold a normal job, and contribute to the evolution of society through greater perception of the mastery within themselves and the shamanic path they have chosen to serve.

Studying Hawaiian Ho'omanamana magic, which is considered to be the technology of consciousness, with a Kahuna always results in experiencing the beauty and power within your Self. It expands your perception of reality from the viewpoint of the Kahuna dedicated to living through the presence of higher consciousness. This is expressed as *Pono* (righteousness), *Aloha* (love, respect, and honor), *Lokahi* (Oneness) and *Mana* (power). Ho'omana Kahiko and Huna teaching comprises knowledge of the intelligence of science, psychology of the mind, philosophy of life, spirituality and religious faith woven into a practical, unified system that describes the relationship of the multi-dimensional nature of humans, God and the universe. The wisdom teachings include:

- **Philosophy of life** as a system of ethics, action and thought guided by Spirit whose focus is resolving the existential questions about the human condition.
- **Transcendentalism** expressing reality as coming from their own limitless thought process; divinity pervades all nature and humanity; progressive views on communal living and feminism are seen through the lens of human goodness.
- **Esoteric** as special knowledge, symbols, myths, religions and the mystical, that lead a person to actual practical application, using both physical and metaphysical senses.
- **Magic** because it works with unseen forces, which are nonetheless real; when principles are followed, it produces results that may not be not fully understood.
- **Metaphysical** because it investigates the fundamental nature and structure of reality.
- **Theological** as the study of specific religious doctrine and theological theories.
- **Theosophy** as the study of God and belief in a deeper spiritual reality, and an interest in occult phenomena.
- **Religion** because it is a particular system of faith and worship that inspires people to attain spiritual perfection and find God within.
- **Science** because it puts intellectual theory into practice in the physical and produces repeatable results.
- **Psychology** because it is the study of the human mind and its functions, especially those affecting behavior in a given context.
- **Universal Truth**, which lies behind all religions and spiritual practice, teaches that God and we are One, there is no separation.
- **Vibration** as a deep inner resonance of the Spirit within, which allows us to connect with the essence of all things.

The Kahuna Religion

The Kahuna religion is higher consciousness spirituality. These beliefs have been handed down from the ancient way (*Ke ala kahiko*) through the family knowledge *(Ohana and Mo'olelo)*. Today, the American Indian Religious Freedom Act also protects Hawaiian religious practices. Religion in the Hawaiian culture was a way of life, which permeated all of ancient society affecting habits, lifestyles, work methods, social policy, and law. The religion was centered through the family and oneness with all things, which inspired people to attain spiritual perfection. Hawaiians believed that the God within was evidential in their Ha (holy) breath. They were in tune with nature, plants, trees, animals, the land, and each other. Kupuna Nana Veary, Hawaiian spiritual leader, describes the religion of the Kahuna:

> "The Hawaiian religion, which I call 'Kahunaism' is a philosophy of everyday life. Stripped of ritual, it is pure metaphysics. The essence of Kahunaism is a deep and genuine reverence for life – living and becoming a part of everything around you. This is what metaphysics teaches and how the Hawaiians live."

The book, *The Kahuna Religion of Hawaii,* is one of the modern accounts of the ancient Hawaiian religion written in 1960, by Daddy Bray, an initiated Kahuna Lapa'au (Healing Priest) of Hawaii. *The Sacred Keys Of The Masters, Ho'omana Kahiko,* was written by Kahu Lanakila Brandt to teach the sacred truths of ancient Hawaiian spirituality. The religious beliefs, practices and principles of the Kahuna, guide the student in spiritual service preparation. They are also an effective guide for personal metaphysical growth for the ordinary person. Hawaiian spirituality honors other religious viewpoints from a deep level of love, compassion and metaphysical insight. Nana Veary was an example of this theological understanding. Nana said:

> "A lot of people have asked, 'What is metaphysics?' I like to say metaphysics is all about love. Love is an innate power you have within you that can change your life. Love is the nature of the inner self, your real self."

From a religious perspective, *Hawaiian Shamanism* is presented from the position that integrates with your present beliefs, providing an opportunity to foster a co-religious point of view. As an example: some Hawaiians practice Christianized versions of the old traditions, while others establish new spiritual practices. Daddy Bray, a Christian Kahuna, explained a new way of integrating with the ancient religions:

> "Christian Kahunas taught a new way of calling the gods. They called it *The Light Way*. Since Kane, Ku, and Lono were so similar to the Trinity, they called upon Jehovah and began their prayers, *E Jehovah*. This was the light way of calling the entire unknown 40,000 and 400 gods. The Christian kahuna ended his prayer, *In Christ we live*."

Many spiritual leaders adopted the Christian teaching linked to their Hawaiian heritage. Leinani Melville predicted that one day the original records upon which Christian fathers founded their religion will be found. It will be a key to open the door leading into their hiding place where a great surprise will come to light. He gave account of the ancient history of Lono that few people know. In *Melville's Esoteric Hawaiian Dictionary* (8-9), he reveals this dramatic research from Hawaiian scholars:

> "Those who possess knowledge of 'The Inner Teaching' know that Christ is the spiritual Lord of the Sun, the same divinity whom the ancient Hawaiian's worshipped by the name of Lono. Christ revealed his spiritual identity to those who are able to hear his message with the inner ear of their spirit, when he transformed himself into the Lord of the Sun and his raiment shone with the light of the sun during his transfiguration upon a mountaintop. The Messiah appeared with his spiritual brothers, whom we know by the names of Moses and Elias. Together they formed the Holy Trinity, and were the Three Princes of Heaven, who were known by the people of Hawaii nei {*beloved Hawaii*} by the names of Lono, Kanaloa, and Ku."

In studying Hawaiian Shamanism, the Kahuna way is not a replacement for your own religious teachings, but it does add dimension and mana to your understanding. It is important to honor the Kahuna religion and study the spiritual traditions to help you understand the commonality of the religion and principles.

> "The Hawaiians do not believe that you should give up your own religion. They believe you should be true to the God in your own heart."
>
> - *The Kahuna Religion of Hawaii* (24)

A large Asian population, together with Western religions, syncretic movements, organizations like the Hawaiian-Christian Hoomana Naauao, branches of the Theosophical Society, Bahai and all emergent spiritual groups established in the islands contribute to a diversity of religious viewpoints. Buddhism has the largest following among these religions, but Shinto, Hinduism, and many other spiritual practices flourish. About half of Hawaii's current residents practice a form of Christianity. Just as every religion is a mixture of other religions and other gods from other cultures, the traditions have been blended with the theological beliefs of the people who settled and founded churches in Hawaii. Most new age and new thought organizations fit into the terms of the religion of kahunaism espoused by Hawaiian elder Nana Veary. The basic metaphysical philosophy encompassed by the older spiritualist ministries like the Universal Church of the Master and newer organizations including the International Metaphysical Ministry, Unity, Science of Mind, Churches of Religious Science, and a myriad of others who teach the same empowered way of living aloha.

Today, the Kahuna religion lives in the practices of devoted Hawaiians as it did in olden times. The cabalistic words, phrases and prayers still serve the priests and theologians as tools for the masters of the culture. The songs of the ancestors are sung, then new prayers and chants are formulated after deep meditation. There is a movement to bring back practices such as La'au Lapa'au (prayer, medicinal plants and herbs to facilitate healing). As cultural knowledge and practices continue to grow in the world, the role of the Kahuna will continue to be treasured.

Chapter 6. Modern Shaman Training

Modern shaman training opportunities extend worldwide, as the expansion of consciousness awakens the healers to unfold their natural shamanic abilities and the call for shamanic service wherever they live. The shaman chooses an awesome path and the training program must be comprehensive to learn every aspect of its mystery. In the old Hawaiian way, the Kahuna was trained solely in how to handle themselves in their own universe, at all times, under all circumstances without the modern aids of pen or computer. According to Abraham Kawaii:

> "In training with Kahuna, there were few words spoken. 95% of instruction was non-verbal. In that way, you had to formulate your own roots. You had to initiate when the time came to initiate. You had to carry forth when the time came to carry forth. You had to know the time. You had to know the time that is within you by way of your feelings. How your body felt would give you the time to move, the time to open your eyes, the time to close your eyes, the time to think about a particular thing, and the time to look intensely at something... and the time all flowed by Spirit..."

The working of Hawaiian shamanism will stay a mystery as long as the search is outside of yourself. You must embark upon your own open-minded re-discovery voyage and begin a fresh start. You must forget what you thought was known and direct the Self (the three Divinities within) to remember, which allows the Soul to work in a new oneness capacity.

Introduction – Modern Shaman Training

Critical to developing kahuna skills is keen observation and awareness of your own self, feelings, beliefs, and patterns. It is the focus for metaphysical instruction and initiatory processes. Shaman training is one in which you must allow your conscious and subconscious minds to gather wisdom from the Higher Self. Manifesting through love and the reality of being in the Divine Presence is the ultimate teacher of modern shaman training. Daddy Bray taught:

> "The purpose behind the kahuna teachings is the revelation of truth within each individual."

Modern shaman training is in essence personal development, and a physiologically based spiritual transformation. To achieve a desired dramatic change includes learning the ancient wisdom and formulating it in such a way that it is applicable in your life and service today. The Kupua shaman training is different from all other preparation in that, although its intent is to communicate wisdom, the real power lies in the connection with the unseen, inner worlds. This includes relationships with angels, guides and ancestors. Unless the haumana (student) accepts this commitment, he or she can only absorb information; the deeper esoteric message will be intellectual theory only, which cannot be implemented fully from the mana the initiate emanates. Dion Fortune, world-renowned Shaman Teacher, depicts this prerequisite:

> "What is required of the neophyte is not a blind obedience but an intelligent comprehension of principles... that he shall have reached such a degree of self-discipline that, when a principle is explained to him, he will immediately be able to put it into practice."

The student must produce evidence of living pono (loving action). When you hear the call to continue on to the deeper levels of Kupua development, explore how to focus on your way of being, your path, and ensure that your movement in the world is not only loving but is also pono in all its forms. The journey starts within you, to tend your own Light and continues for you to employ the same quality in all your actions. This means that you must do the work internally to maximize external results.

Personal Consciousness Development

Personal consciousness development is part of tending the inner Light and transmitting appropriate physical action. Instructional guidelines for social behavior and for acceptable shaman/client relationships are drawn and taught in shamanic preparation. Guidelines should be reviewed and exercises investigated for relevance. Exploration of both internal and external information is fertile ground for personal growth. Built upon a creative strategy, personal growth is where the fountain of the magic flows or rather where the magic is being developed within your three selves.

Your responsibility for functioning in consciousness presents multiple opportunities for expression. Your experiences range from your activity in the very grossest density, which create your BS (belief systems) in drama and trauma. Interaction in the higher energies develops love and light, where it is easy to express aloha/pono behavior. The quality of your personal consciousness nucleus always depends upon the level of consciousness in which you choose to engage. A shaman, just like any other person, can only demonstrate the amount of love and express integrity of behavior at the level of consciousness from which he or she functions. Spiritual and physical action will always be expressed from that level ... no higher and no lower.

Personal development of the shaman is governed by the maturity and spiritual growth gained through consciousness encounters. The flow of mana is reflected in lovingness and is expressed as pono behavior. Thus, the real preparation to ensure readiness for service is through the work of consciousness expansion. A shaman must be prepared to move through all energies with grace and ease to meet the needs of the shamanic service offered professionally. When the goal of the shaman is to demonstrate personal higher consciousness growth and be able to raise or lower these levels at will, the dynamics of consciousness flows as a vibrant, automatic program. The Masters point to the state of expanded consciousness, which is measured as value choices and in terms of consciousness evaluating systems.

Modern Consciousness Values System

Mana flow can be identified by how your consciousness is demonstrated through what you value and how it is prioritized in your life. This is helpful for the modern shaman who functions in the role of personal and/or corporate management consulting. It is useful in family dynamics that bring understanding to the variety of value systems, which may also vary dramatically within the family group. The operating consciousness of individuals can be compared in relationship to each other and the group's overall energetics. Pono (right action) is evaluated through these same levels or stages of consciousness in varying degrees of expression.

Most theories map consciousness in a format that describe different stages, some more complex than others. The goal is to comprehend the movement in and between stages of consciousness expression. More abstract facets are viewed as tiered consciousness beliefs, which describe characteristics of insightfulness or as the ability to live in pono right action expressed through social traditions. As a practitioner, not only is it important to know your own personal consciousness level, it is also imperative to know the level of consciousness and value systems in which the client operates.

Nine Visible Levels of Consciousness

There are nine major visible consciousness fields and within each stage, there are 49 planes revealing an opportunity for an in-depth view of soul-growth, which produces a formidable evolutionary frequency. This perspective reveals overall growth in levels that identify the nuances of consciousness behavior as it moves toward a fuller mana actualization. This postulates evolving consciousness that takes place in the PEMS (physical, emotional, mental, and spiritual) through expanding the power of personal mastery. Conscious evolution increases the capacity of the individual to gather, receive, store, and use mana in the body to consistently flow and function in the manner described below. The Consciousness Levels 1-9 Summary is a review of each consciousness level, identifying what it governs, and the purpose of the beliefs.

Consciousness Levels 1 – 9 Summary

1. Life Force Consciousness:
Governs: Reactive survival in the physical dimension.
Purpose: Subconscious mind controls the seat of physical vitality and fundamental urges. Conscious mind builds a physical foundation to establish the material environment.

2. Awakening Consciousness:
Governs: Articulation of aspects of selves in relationships.
Purpose: Conscious mind stimulates the awakening processes.

3. Individual Consciousness:
Governs: Egocentric balance in self and interactions.
Purpose: Individual learns to assert him or herself in a group. To be in control of self and have sufficient self-esteem. He or she overcomes passivity and indecisiveness to obtain what is desired.

4. Transforming Consciousness:
Governs: Love and loyalty; learns to play well with others.
Purpose: Create love, kindness and affection demonstrating your compassion, friendliness and establish harmonious relationships with family and community.

5. Achievist Consciousness:
Governs: Creating in higher levels of awareness.
Purpose: Transcend first four levels in conscious physical, emotional, mental and spiritual interaction.

6. Personal Consciousness:
Governs: Higher Self-expression in conscious mind.
Purpose: Higher consciousness mana self-expression is used to impact human well-being.

7. Planetary Consciousness:
Governs: Personal responsibility and global life quality.
Purpose: Raise your consciousness from a local to a global level of interconnectedness.

8. Integrative Consciousness:
Governs: Broader goals of an integrative perspective.

Purpose: Live from the Soul every day to integrate the physical, emotional, mental and spiritual in balance.

9. Systemic Soul Consciousness:
Governs: Conceptual expansion of conscious physical systems by refinement of emotional, mental, and spiritual empowerment.
Purpose: Enlightenment that functions in all awareness of Universal Mind Consciousness in daily life to clear and uplift.

Consciousness Evolution

The purpose of consciousness evolution is to function fully in all levels of consciousness. All stages of consciousness flow through the three selves and function in all levels of realities. The teachings of the Kupua are ever evolving as the consciousnesses of individuals evolve. An aspiration of most Kupua is to have the capacity and expertise to work with any and all systems.

Since consciousness is a living, breathing force, it streams naturally through the ebb and flow of thoughts and actions every moment of every day. The path to enlightenment is not strictly an upward ladder, although you may view developing Kupua skills as an overall evolution of consciousness. As individuals, we are working in all of these categories every day. As we grow and have greater capacity to use higher consciousness, our consciousness advances. We have more experiences that allow us to go to our really authentic place, and our horizons open to reveal a different operating capacity.

Consciousness frequency oscillates more like the currents of the air. This means that everyone doesn't necessarily move from a lower level straight through each level until the highest is reached (as if climbing a ladder). Just as air currents have freedom to swirl in all directions, different facets of the physical, mental, emotional and spiritual dynamics register on their own mixed consciousness frequencies. With this mixture of demands, there is always a chance to gain mana or lose mana with every thought and action taken. Thus, the capacity to generate, convey, and use Divine Consciousness is always available whether you connect to it or not.

People who practice aloha consistently, for instance, have the capacity to express a higher degree of usable mana flow in most things they do because they consistently function in a higher consciousness venue. On the other hand, a person who lives a good life but has a drinking problem with exploding anger issues will have outbursts of unloving behavior and will be incapable of expressing pono actions consistently. Higher consciousness living resulting in the ability to function in loving pono actions is a choice. It is all a matter of choosing where you want to be in consciousness and if you are dedicated to living a pono life. You have the ability to change the consciousness level of past stored memories each time you remember or recount an incident. The memory will appear as empowering or disempowering, according to your present state of consciousness choice. In this respect, you have the opportunity to live the situations over many times. You change the level of consciousness in any way you want to remember it each time you respond to the memory of the experience.

The Sacred Bowl of Light

The Kahuna Kupua initiate needs to learn about the Sacred Bowl of Light if unknown. In ancient times, the people knew they carried the Light within themselves and attended it faithfully. In *Tales from the Night Rainbow* (18-19), Pali Jae Lee and Koko Willis transcribed the story (*mo'olelo*) from Kaili'ohe Kame'ekua:

Mo'olelo o na Po Makole

> "Each child born has at birth, a Bowl of Perfect Light. If he tends his Light it will grow in strength and he can do all things – swim with the shark, fly with the birds, know and understand all things. If, however, he becomes envious or jealous, he drops a stone into his Bowl of Light and some of the Light goes out. Light and the stone cannot hold the same space. If he continues to put stones in the Bowl of Light, the Light will go out

and he will become a stone. A stone does not grow, nor does it move. If at any time he tires of being a stone, all he needs to do is turn the bowl upside down and the stones will fall away and the Light will grow once more."

We are connected to the Divine by energetic vortexes, which create the Sacred Bowl of Light. There are three Pikos (centers) located on the top of the head, navel and genital areas. These receptor/receivers connect the Sacred Bowl of Light to the Divine. The Piko Po'o (crown of the head) connects a person's spirit or soul to the spiritual realm; the Piko Weana or navel (umbilical) connects to their parents in the present; and the Piko Ma'i (genitals) connects a person to future generations.

Renew the Sacred Bowl of Light

The first step is to attend to your Sacred Bowl of Light. Initiation into mystical preparation is to empty out the stones in your Bowl of Light and restore the illumination (*a'o*). It is good to choose action from the symbolic world by literally finding a bowl and filling it with rocks. Conduct ceremony to empty your bowl and cleanse your personal bowl of light in any and preferably all levels of reality after it is empty. It is always appropriate to clear unwanted energies or transmute them into usable mana for you to regain and maintain self-balance. Learn how to clear and tend your Light. Become more knowledgeable about yourself and do the work.

Attention must be drawn to provide the activation of the Sacred Light. In other words, it is not enough for the initiate to operate from the emptiness of a bowl turned upside down, but it must be from the restored Light to fill and carry it forward if others are to be ignited from its flame. When the Light of your bowl is dimmed, take steps to renew it. The Aligning Light of La'akea (God Light) clears, cleanses, and restores the Light within. After renewal, the Light must be maintained in spiritual integrity if you are prepared in the ancient tradition to be in service as a Carrier of the Light. It is up to you whether you are in pono or choose to be without. Claim the blessings of the sacred light.

E ho'omaika'i i kea la'a kea me ke aloha mau loa
Blessings of sacred light and everlasting love

The Challenge of Personal Growth

The challenge of personal growth is in developing emotional, mental and spiritual interactions of pono. The shaman must understand the philosophy of human development from the perspective of functioning in the lower dimensions through the full spectrum of higher consciousness response and behavior. This means that the shaman seeks knowledge of all stages of consciousness development. The mastery of living from the self-greatness within is at the very core of shamanic life and service. The categories of consciousness expressions identify the progression of overcoming negative thoughts and actions in the three stages of development from the lowest to the highest pono interactions. This scale offers the key to moving from density by functioning with the qualities of courage, neutrality, and willingness that establish the habits of acceptance and reason. Recognize the qualities in yourself and others as outlined below:

1. Emotional Reactions Serving In Density

When you demonstrate any of the emotional traits shown here, you are functioning in the lowest debilitating consciousness levels of density where drama and trauma becomes the focus:

- Shame, guilt, apathy, grief, fear, desire, anger, and pride

2. Bridging Out Of Density

This density consciousness functioning level is a bridge from the lower into higher. It includes the ability to release the lower density and connect to the higher realms. It confers emotional, mental, and spiritual growth. Coping mechanisms and aptitudes emerge to empower lovingness and serve others through these three vehicles that transform emotions:

- Courage, neutrality, and willingness

3. Functioning In Higher Consciousness

This is the level in which aloha and pono can be expressed. It is the higher consciousness standard Hawaiian Shamanism demands, and the level in which it is necessary to function, in order to perform the spiritual work. These steps also lead toward the development of enlightenment:

- Acceptance, reason, love, joy, and peace

Understand Your Self

> "As soon as you understand that your real self is the God in your heart, then there is no obstacle to your success. This is because we are all part of God. How can we understand God unless we know the part of God that is in us?"
>
> - *The Kahuna Religion of Hawaii* (24)

Alignment with the higher Self within feels different for each person, but the result is the same. You know you are in alignment when your heart feels open and your body feels comfortable. The purpose of it all is to know the loving self within, and to see all interactions as positive opportunities to learn and grow within all relationships. That sounds easy; it is, if you allow yourself to grow, not only to expand in consciousness, but also to take action from your own inner prompting. What you seek is within. Each person must find his or her own way in the consciousness chosen from moment to moment. Ancient and modern wisdom teachers agree: "Look within, for there is where you will find your selves." Kahu David Bray taught:

> "God is understanding the positive emotions, which lead to Divine knowledge and attract health attitudes and the Au'makua of creativity discovery within us."

E Nana I Ke Kumu - To look to the Source Within

Focus upon the Source Within yourself. Your understanding of yourself is what ultimately transforms. If you get stuck behind a veil that covers your true essence, it leaves you flailing about with the idea that you are "not enough." The ancestors used the saying *Nana I Ke Kumu* often, as a means of educating the youth to seek answers from within and encouraged them to learn from the wise elderly (*Kupuna*). Daddy Bray said:

> "Our understanding of ourselves is what ultimately transforms us. As we come to know ourselves. To be at peace and at home within ourselves, we reach out and understand the greater whole."

We must also find ourselves in the study of nature itself with all its wisdom that is portrayed in the forest and streams, the ocean with all its life and the air that keeps it alive. When lost, check your hokulea (mental star compass) to find your way. Sail past any old shackles that limit and take you off course. Cultivating your emotional intelligence is a significant part of staying on course. Emotional intelligence is the ability to identify, understand, and manage your own emotions and influence the emotions of others. Growth in this area also assures the development of intrapersonal skills necessary to understand yourself deeply. Interpersonal skill is a critical expertise needed to understand and adequately facilitate troubled people effectively. The initiate needs to develop both interpersonal and intrapersonal abilities. Intrapersonal skill is the capacity to understand yourself, while interpersonal skill is the ability to comprehend others. These are essential areas to accentuate for personal and professional effectiveness:

- ***Self-Awareness*** – The ability to recognize and understand your moods, emotions and drives, as well as their effect on others

- ***Self-Regulation*** – The ability to control or re-direct disruptive impulses and moods and the propensity to suspend judgment and think before acting

- **Motivation** – A passion to work for reasons that go beyond money and status and a propensity to pursue goals with energy and persistence

- **Social Skills** – A proficiency in managing relationships and building networks

- **Empathy** – The ability to comprehend and experience the emotions of other people

The Practice of Aloha

Aloha is the powerful practice behind mystical skills. The steps moving from apprentice to practitioner demand the continued progression through the discipline of aloha practices. Pono must be mastered through the ability to gather, process and express harmony and balance. Laura Kealoha Yardley teaches:

> "...The vibration of 'aloha' is Spirit manifesting through love. The concept of 'aloha' is being in the presence of Spirit"

The Kupua practice, in the ancient sense, offers a loving way to work with Spirit that is unique and heals. It is one thing to talk about philosophy, it is quite another to take steps to actually practice the laws of aloha. Living with the power of aloha is not by accident. Kahuna Hale Makua outlines three sacred laws of aloha to ensure an abundant flow of life.

1) Love All that you see with Humility.
2) Live All that you feel with Reverence.
3) Know All that you possess with Discipline.

The Kupua learns to put love into action. This means to bless every person, place, and thing, including yourself. In addition, it means that you must stop participating in negative thoughts and activity. When you criticize people, you are actually cursing them. The practice of aloha is simple, yet not consistently easy. It is the one practice that will transform your life and the lives of others. Kupua mystical training follows the description of the meaning of Kupua. You must use aloha to:

- Unfold from the highest Source
- Emerge from your shell
- Sprout from the seed within
- Develop
- Grow
- Expand into the fullness of life

Metaphysically, you are an offspring of Spirit (a supernatural being). The secret is to emanate from Spirit into physical loving action. If you don't master this ability, think twice about becoming a shaman because you can wreak havoc on yourself and others if you don't anchor this quality from the very highest perspective.

Perpetuating the Light of Your Spirit

In the practice of aloha, there is a natural progression of physical loving action that fills your Bowl, which is the process of perpetuating the Light of your Spirit. Delve deeply into the meaning that Hank Wesselman relayed from Kahuna Kupua Makua's message in *The Bowl of Light: Ancestral Wisdom* in order to find the truth within yourself. The foundation of Hawaiian thinking is this circular and interlinking shamanic mana flow you can create, as well as receive, in the practice of perpetuating the Light of your Spirit:

- Love all that you see: In order to love all that you see, you must come from a place of humility.

- Live in a state of humility: When you live in a state of humility, you must connect with compassion. This allows you to experience the power of aloha.

- With the power of aloha, live all that you feel: When you live what you sense and feel through aloha, it leads into reverence, which activates value and acceptance.

- Practice acceptance: The practice of acceptance shows

respect for everyone and everything you encounter. You begin to evaluate your own motivations and actions through self-examination.

- Self-examination: When you know all that you possess including what possesses you, your self-discipline or lack of it is revealed.

- Self-discipline: When you use self-discipline you are able to walk the sacred path to discover who you are.

- Know who you are: When you know who you are, you have the mana to live in lovingness, to love yourself and others, which ignites and fills your Bowl of Light.

These steps are necessary for truly living aloha in the ancient tradition, which is acceptance of love, enriched by tenderness, compassion, consideration, humility, understanding and a self-disciplined life. The Kahuna has the power that nothing can take away. It has relevance and is the power of aloha; it conveys the ability to shine the Light into darkness no matter how dark it may seem to be. Kupua training emphasizes these three standards:

- Purity of integrity
- Clarity of intent
- Application of knowledge

The Aloha Spirit

The ancients nurtured the teachings and daily practices of Oneness in unconditional love as the *Aloha Spirit*. Pilahi Paki said, "The Aloha Spirit is the coordination of the mind and heart… it's within the individual. It brings you down to yourself. You must think and emote good feelings to others." Beloved Kahu Lanakila Brandt exemplified aloha qualities. He described aloha as a meaningful expression of the spirit and said:

> "…Although the word is Hawaiian, its message is universal… love, enriched by tenderness, compassion, consideration, charity, and understanding. To me, aloha is that innate quality, which permits us, whatever our

circumstances, to revel in the inalienable wealth with which our benevolent gods have endowed us; to luxuriate in the heady fragrance of lush mountain groves as we chant paeans of love to 'Earth Mother' Haumea while harvesting fragrant ferns, lichens, and sweet maile vines to adorn the hula altar of divine Laka.

It is communicating with, and receiving inner guidance from the earth, sea, the winds, and the sky, from the creatures that swim, crawl, and walk. It is treading precipitous and often bizarre lava footpaths down into the fiery heart of Pele's Kilauea home – to dance and chant and lay our humble nature offerings upon the molten robes of our adored fire goddess.

Aloha, for me, is sharing the deep knowledge of our Hawaiian ancestors with the truly dedicated tide of Seekers whose mystic helmsman guide them to our beacon light each year. It is sharing with the many enchanting public presence, lovingly honed skills, and the passionate spiritual expression of my sacred dancers, the women of my halau hula.

Aloha is a complex and important word of near unlimited powers. But its greatest power and beauty is that, by whatever name, we all have it! We need only to open the floodgates and let it flow; let it inundate all within our individual spheres. Then truly will each of us be living within that internal paradise, the Spirit of Aloha."

The Deeper Meaning of Aloha

Insight into the practice of aloha can be obtained by studying the teaching held within the five letters of aloha. Some of these spiritual laws of the foundation of aloha are:

A: *Ala* is to wake up; watchful alertness. It is consciousness of all seeing awareness. Omniscience. Be empowered with '*Ala*: being watchful. Hold within yourself the divine nature of *Ke Akua* (God) in all existence. *Akua* helps you understand the hidden mysteries of the universe. After awakening, how to access mana is discovered through the value of *Alo*: share the

Divine breath of life face-to-face. Breathe higher consciousness with *Akahai*: Grace, kindness to express with tenderness.

L: *Lokahi* is the principle of unity; express with the harmony of oneness. *Aloha/Lokahi* love is the inherent unity of oneness. Roots *lo'o, ka, hi* and *kahi* contain the philosophy of Lokahi, which is to obtain unity of Mind, Body and Spirit in the human form. Live in harmony with the order of the universe. *Mana* of Lokahi achieves a higher state of oneness that finds God in all.

O: *Oiaio* is truthful honesty. *Oia* (truth) and *I'o* (substantive essence) translate as absolute or plain truth. Mana is applied as *Olu'olu*: Gentle; agreeable to express with pleasantness. O: what is felt inside manifests on the external.

H: *Ha'aha'a* is the deepest humility and unpretentiousness; emotion (passion) of Spirit energizing the human experience. *Ha*: the heart and power of aloha is the breath of God; radiant energy essential to life. *Ha ha*: breath of the four male deities.

A: *Ahonui* patience expressed with perseverance is formed from *aho* (breath) and *nui* (great) or *loa* (highest). Ahonui describes sacred breathing used to prepare for rituals, prayer or meditation. Aloha action means "the breath of God in me, greets the breath of God in you." Aloha lives through these deeds:

- Connect to God, Angels, Guides, and Ancestors
- Awareness of and the ability to direct the powers of mind and the forces of nature
- Connect to the High Self and integrate the inner selves in ritual and in daily life
- Learn and live the principles of the teachings from antiquity that work in the world today
- Master the levels of reality and use them in practices of healing, counseling, and teaching life skills
- Connect to and use all forms of energies as mana
- Attain, maintain and teach wisdom in the world

Personal Development Plan For Aloha Practice

A personal development plan for an aloha practice includes spiritual preparation and service. In its most basic form, it means practicing loving right action. This requires cultivating compassion, love, mercy, affection, and peace emphasizing accepting and forgiving yourself and others. The first priority referenced by Nana Veary is:

> "Prepare your mind to receive the best that life has to offer. Become increasingly aware of the one presence, the one life, the one spirit, which is God. All sense of lack or limitation should have no place in your consciousness. Everything is possible to you according to your acceptance, and the way spirit works through your belief."

Cultivate Positive Emotional Virtues

Emotional virtues are a vital part of the aloha preparation. In practice, it means giving more than you receive and being willing to show others kindness through action, even in the smallest forms. Kahuna Bray and Douglas Low developed this self-evaluation checklist to assess your emotional virtues growth:

A. Humbleness
B. Patience
C. Self-Control
D. Perseverance
E. Kindness
F. Tolerance
G. Remain undisturbed by obstacles, delay or failure
H. Patience and fairness with those whose opinions and practices differ from yours
I. Bear stress and strain
J. Exercise love and calmness at all times
K. Meditate on the Divine nature of the soul
L. Openness to reality
M. Understanding the four great elements of life and their interaction to form all processes
N. Realization of eternal life in the reality of God

Essential to the practicing of aloha, is the idea that all of us are given the transcendental tools to think for ourselves, make right choices and find or create ways to heal ourselves and others.

The Practice of Aloha To-Do List:

1. Express more gratitude in your life.
2. Bless everyone and everything with humility.
3. Create positive living.
4. Cultivate optimism.
5. Believe that if it can happen, it will.
6. Create winning.
7. Stimulate the intellectual side of yourself.
8. Practice acts of loving-kindness.
9. Make everything you do an excuse for creating love.
10. Nurture social relationships.
11. Create deep, meaningful relationships.
12. Develop skills to change disruptive non-pono behaviors.
13. Forgive yourself and others for things real and imagined.
14. Increase mana flow experiences.
15. Be empowered as many times during the day as possible.
16. Eliminate mana-depleting activities.
17. Slow down every day to smell the roses. Appreciate life.
18. Set goals and be committed to achieve the best you can.
19. Focus attention upon what you are led to do.
20. Create a healthy mental outlook.
21. Cultivate emotional, intelligent healthy patterns.
22. Partake in fun physical endeavors.
23. Stimulate sex and sensuality.
24. Live your life to achieve the goal of your incarnation.

Aloha Healing Format

The practice of aloha is the format for healing and entry into the deeper spiritual pursuits. Po'oKahuna had the power to heal through prayer and faith because they had *Ike* (spiritual power), which they transmitted to others. Daddy Bray taught that the deeper you go spiritually, the higher you must go into the material energy to spread your ike into the world. This is outlined in *The Kahuna Religion of Hawaii* (24):

> "The unity of the Spiritual and the Material is like a light bulb that cannot fill a room with its glow unless there is a current of positive and negative electricity. Light is produced by a flow of the positive and negative energy. The same is true of a person. The Material and Spiritual go together. The person who balances those two forces has a strong foundation. He succeeds in life."

In a 1988 interview in the *Los Angeles Whole Life Times, Masters of Hawaiian "Magic,"* Abraham Kawaii said that the basic principle of the art that he practiced is an encompassing one. It is the spiritual understanding that everything is related to everything. In this view, everything gets refined every moment of your life. It is the magical realism that all events are not isolated and random. Everything relates to each other. He said:

> "It might be difficult for the modern world to understand that ancient people were concerned with molecular and atomic realms. The concerns that particular domain being the cellular structure and even further into the molecular and atomic. The sub-gods were basically names of what you know now to be molecules and atoms. Therefore, the Kahunas were able to change structure by attuning themselves to these sub-gods, having a communication with these sub-gods to be able to do a bone healing instantly or to be able to change or move matter. The concept of the Kahuna in looking at anything is that there is a being within a being. Worlds within worlds, spheres with spheres, lives within lives, universes within universe."

Functioning from these beliefs, Hawaiian methods of healing bring into focus the ability to change structures of the mind, body, and spirit. The need in the world today is to live the life of a healer in this deeper knowledge. It is a call to enter into a new realm of magic and miracles. Training must include the integration of the spiritual and material worlds. In doing so, understand and appreciate who you are, where all things have come from, and how all things can be affected by either movement of thought, word, or action. Techniques can be learned through these Hawaiian shamanic vehicles:

1. Direct experience.
2. Explanations when the student can demonstrate them.
3. Questions are partially answered when the student pieces together information through constant questioning.
4. Classes are taught to groups in order to pass the traditions to as many people as possible.
5. Student responsibility is to participate by demonstrating what they have learned.

Find Your Healing Space

Find your healing space within yourself and your place of service. Be healing in everything you do. Lessen the gap between the intentional healing work you do, words you speak, and the actions you take daily. Follow your inner inspiration to find where healing opportunities appeal to you. Here are some places where healing Light is needed in the world:

- Teaching: Speaking, instructing, training, counseling, writing, publishing, and distributing information
- Individual: Any direct client or patient-centered therapy based on Hawaiian shamanism
- Group Therapy: Ho'oponopono, and peacemaking
- Dream Interpretation: Growth, revelation and counseling
- Eco-therapy: Any form of healing the environment or human relationships with the environment
- Kokua/Aloha Groups: Form and/or direct Healing Circles, Blessing alliances, similar, and community support groups that extend loving help to those in need
- Ministry - informal or ordained: Function as independent or pastoral clergy, give spiritual and practical counseling to individuals, couples, families, and children in all areas
- Living Pono: Extend pono in word, thought, and deed
- Kokua: Loving, sacrificial help to others for their benefit
- Everywhere is a place for healing and renewal

Chapter 7. Modern Shaman Mysticism

Modern shamanic mysticism is a spiritual composite that moves beyond the physical body, which influences life through an empowering metaphysical connection. The shaman perceives direct knowledge or experience of Divine presence. He or she intuitively connects with areas of modern life in appropriate levels of consciousness, in order to use the dimensional energies to bring healing and change to people, places, and situations. According to the *Merriam-Webster* Dictionary, the word modern comes from the Latin *modo* meaning just now, and from *modus* meaning measure. Modern is defined as that which relates to the present and may involve recent techniques, methods, and ideas. Because the modern shaman communicates his or her mystical experiences through present day culture, religion, and technology, the individual accesses global consciousness, blending a more expansive view of oneself and the world. A modern practitioner knows the universal mystical reality of the past, as well as the present. It is the source behind all creation and holds a purposeful focus upon the present moment. When the Mystic observes matter, it is not solid at all. Beneath it all, it actually consists of electrons and protons swirling in a fluid magnetic field. Understanding of the universe changes as technology progresses. It is up to the modern Mystic to share how the Divine manifests in the present day scientific knowledge. One definition is:

> "A modern-day Mystic is someone who practices mysticism and will utilize present day interpretations, innovations, techniques, methods, and expanded ideas."

It is common for a student to study with many different Kahuna to hone their skills in a variety of ancient beliefs and healing arts. Many people who are attracted to the philosophy and spiritual practices of Polynesia have had past lives as Kahuna or priestly connections. They may have participated in various spiritual traditions that created innate mystical power and shaman craft abilities. It is this deeply spiritual aspect of modern shamanism that naturally flows into the mystical expansion of the initiate.

The Modern Shaman Initiate – Ho'omaka

The shaman initiate is called *Ho'omaka*. The root of the word means to cause envisioning, revealing in the Light, as when a flower opens to unfold its center; to cast a glow; and as when the expression in one's eyes reveals the spark of thoughts within. An initiate develops talents and abilities from the dimensions within their own self, like the maturing into a magnificent rose. The ho'omaka initiation process happens by connecting to Source.

Everyone receives initiations as a part of their life path shifting from one phase into the next, which feeds the unfolding process. There are also times when initiations happen that just feel as if we are greatly inspired. Some people are slow burners and only notice it as time to put on "the shoes." Others may notice that you have developed an extraordinary ability to perceive certain information beyond usual awareness. The initiate develops powers of perception that seem to come from a superhuman source – yet is absolutely normal when working in higher awareness using concepts and principles as well as multiple reality connections in the Divine mana flow.

Kupua Transformation

The Kupua creates transformation by following universal laws that are formulas for success. By expanding the conscious mind, the Kupua not only thinks logically but also functions from a sense of deep knowingness, which is referred to as *ulukau* (intuition). By intuition we mean: Intuition is the immediate and direct acquisition of an idea, feeling, or essence of a thing, without the intermediate service of words or data. On a higher plane, intuition may be referred to as the "mystical vision or experience." Some of the best answers to the mysteries of life have come from poets or prophets in moments of mystical awareness.

In a higher consciousness concept, intuition is the psychological/spiritual, which combines with an intellectual approach to discern reality. No conceptualizing, synthesizing, rationalizing, inductive or deductive reasoning are involved. Kupua intuition takes place in the state of "knowingness" - no tedious hypothesizing, testing and gathering of data is necessary. These thought processes may or may not have preceded or prepared the way for the current insight to occur. In the ancient traditions of Hawaii, when intuition and intellect were used in the highest state of consciousness, it was the result of various disciplines of awareness, which include but are not limited to:

- Pule – Prayer, Haipule – activate prayer as a state of being
- Ha Breath – activates a higher state of being
- No'ono'o – meditation
- Hakalau - Expanded Awareness
- Akakua – Trance as a normal state of being
- Temple Healing – Lomi Lomi, Kahi Loa
- Kilokilo – Divination for self and others
- Ho'ike na ka po – Revelatory dream

Shapeshifting

One mystical aspect of Kupua is in Shapeshifting. There is much misunderstanding about shapeshifting perpetuated by those who don't understand it and cannot conceive of it being anything but conjecture. Shapeshifting is a naturally occurring ability that everyone possesses at some level. For instance: As the body ages, it shifts energy affecting the physical body shape. However, this skill is also a part of the shaman's bag that shifts energy with purpose instantly.

> "In mythology, folklore and speculative fiction, shape-shifting (or metamorphosis) is the ability of a being or creature to completely transform its physical form or shape. This is usually achieved through an inherent ability of a mythological creature, divine intervention, or the use of magic."
>
> – *Shapeshifting, Wikipedia*

We are energy beings and energy shifts for a reason. The truth is that energy shifts dramatically via the emotions and intellect, resulting in a change in the body, mind, and spirit. In actuality, shapeshifting *is* metamorphosis (shifting of energy) in one sense or another. For example, shapeshifting takes place in life through the emotional attitudes, which may be expressions of joy, happiness, anger, fear, and any emotional projections or intuitive interactions. Body shape change takes place as a natural occurrence. However, deep body morphing often happens more slowly than the widely touted quick methods in stories.

According to your connection, a shifting of energy always takes place when you are in touch with another person, place, or thing, or when another person, place, or thing is in touch with you. Everyone has the ability to sense and feel others at some degree. During an intensely moving actor's performance an internal and external mental manipulation takes place. The actor projects emotional energy. The audience responds to the actor's shifting of energy by internalizing or externalizing from the stimuli. Actors and audience may feel the shifting of energy and/or experience physical metamorphosis. When such episodes occur, your face may take on a slightly different shape; your body may feel different and/or even look different; and your speech may be unlike how you normally speak. These changes may occur with a sudden onset that is quite noticeable. So, what causes the shapeshifting? This kind of shapeshifting takes place because there is an "energy shift" in an individual, whether it takes place from an internal or external influence.

Mediumship Shapeshifting

A shifting of energy takes place in Mediumship Shapeshifting because Mediumship is the ability to be at one (or is an embodiment) with the spirit of another person, place or thing (whether living or dead). Pukui (1972:46) observed that an aumakua could enter the body and speak through a spiritual medium called a Haka. People, spirits, angels, guides, and ancestors transmit their energy. Thus, you see what they see; hear what they hear; feel or sense the same way; or speak for them, and sometimes speak as if you *are* them. All things within the realm of mediumship may shift energy so much that not only do you look, speak or act differently, you also have extended perception to be able to know, experience, and perceive time and space through the senses of the other. When the medium transmits this energy, it may bring metamorphosis to others as when healing takes place. Another type of mediumship is a channeling or conscious observation of mediumship communication, which is not an experience of oneness that brings about a metamorphosis for the medium. It can, however, bring about the same transmittal of energy and effect changes as in Spirit Possession Mediumship.

Shapeshifting can be accomplished in any level of reality. As long as the universal laws' pertaining to the framework of each reality is followed, great success can be obtained that benefit the practitioner as well as others. The advanced spiritual shapeshifter can utilize the knowledge of mysticism to obtain amazing results. Not understanding the subtle forces of nature and the etheric, the mass mind of nearly all ages tends to regard mediumistic powers with awe. The medium, as a bridge to the unknown, is at times regarded with fear, veneration, and even with hatred, which breeds an atmosphere of religious prejudice and profound ignorance of the subtle Universal Laws of the Mind. However, for the well-informed and dedicated individual, the supernatural and its empowerment is revealed and available to create the magic known to the Kupua shapeshifter.

Aumakua Shapeshifting

In Hawaiian mythology, the deification and transfiguration of ancestors into aumakua was a part of their Hawaiian heritage. The family communicated with aumakua as trusted advisors and healers. As family members, the aumakua had a loving concern for their descendants and acted as guardians. They would often assume their aumakua body to communicate a warning of impending catastrophe. Aumakua could shapeshift into the form of animals, places, rocks, or people to intervene or to save their descendants from harm. Thus, ancient Hawaiians believed in a powerful spirit being able to appear as all four, switching from form to form as convenient. This explains the ability of the Kupua Kamapua'a who had the capability to possess many different body forms and dimensional depths. It also depicts the same multidimensional qualities all people possess to shapeshift mentally, emotionally, and physically.

Empathic Shapeshifting

Empathic shapeshifting is an ability to understand another's perspective and entails a sensitivity to other people's feelings and emotions. Humans *are* empathic and many are so much so that they cannot tell their own energy from that of another. There is a subtle vibrational difference that those who are sensitive can discern when they are fully present. An empathic person will sense the higher vibrations of appreciation, peace, and love, which affect upliftment, and healing. When vibrations of anger, fear, guilt, shame and blame are acutely felt, the response is an immediate downshifting, which may become an overwhelming, intense negativity. Feelings of apprehension or aggression may turn into harmful and detrimental influence. Without being aware of this empathic shapeshifting, vibrations affect everyone because emotions are exchanged in sympathetic agreement.

Humans have the natural ability to connect on a Soul level with each other. A trained empath can feel or sense the field of another in need. Thus, attuned to it, they resonate a higher frequency, which the recipient can use to a desired purpose. Shapeshifting at the intellectual level affects a state of mental empowerment, which reinforces freedom of thought. Shapeshifting at the emotional level is a force behind true healing and supports others to attain their full potential.

Chapter 8. Shaman Principles

Introduction to Kupua Shaman Principles

Kupua Shaman principles express a profound simplicity for loving and holding a reverence for all of life. The seven principles expressed by Serge King (modern adaptation) and Daddy Bray's sixty-eight (Ancient wisdom), describe higher shamanic path of enlightenment. The primary focus of the Hawaiian way is to live in the oneness of God-consciousness and follow principles to live life fully connected in harmony and balance. The principles of Hawaiian shamanism reveal who we are as human beings. We *are* first and foremost consciousness and are choosing to have reality experiences in which we take on a kino (body form).

The Western world wants to approach shaman knowledge from a physical position and seeks to comprehend the metaphysical influence upon it. The material world seeks to evolve *into* higher consciousness, hoping to find their capacity to create life from the highest spiritual level, not realizing it already exists within them. This begins a tug of war between the spiritual and the material approach. The battle becomes to either live in the oneness of spirit or take the position of separateness in the density of matter.

From the perspective of Hawaiian thinking, the truth is: We *are Higher Consciousness*. The principles of Hawaiian Shamanism provide guidance to live in the duality of earth while functioning as the true higher consciousness Self. The Kupua principles in this book are divided into these three segments:

1. Qualities of Consciousness: Qualities teach the ability with which to live life in higher purpose.
2. Operating Principles: Seven operating principles describe how to implement the inner knowledge and live it.
3. Creating Realities: The eighth principle instructs how to create reality out of realities through Ho'omanamana.

Qualities of Consciousness

The capacity for connecting with the Divine with deep feeling, or emotions stirring healing energy are defining qualities of higher consciousness. Featured here are a few qualities gleaned from my Hawaiian teachers that express the action of the principles of higher consciousness ho'omanamana. To summarize:

Expressions of Consciousness Qualities

- Aloha: Spirit manifesting through love
- Aloha 'aina: Love, respect, honor, and care for the land
- Ho'o maika'i: Bless, thank, acceptance, praise, improve
- Ho'okipa: Hospitality, sharing, honoring others
- Ho'oulu: Time of becoming, growth of knowledge, hope
- Ho'oponopono: Make right, create harmony and balance, restore perfection in relationships
- Kala: Untie the knots, cleanse, free each other
- Kokua: Help, assist, support without being asked
- Koru: Represents evolution as humans
- Kupuna: Respect and care for elders, they carry wisdom
- Laulima: Many hands working together, cooperation
- Lokahi: Act in harmony and create oneness/unity
- Mahalo: Appreciation, gratitude, thanks
- Malama: Radiation of Light, Divine Source Illumination
- Mihi: Confession, repent, apologize, forgive completely
- Ohana: Family, the community and extended family
- Pono: Act correctly, right action, in perfect order

Operating Kupua Principles

The people who remember who they are do not need principles in which to operate. The principles are written for people who do not know or do not thoroughly understand the higher consciousness ways of the ancient traditions, or how the people perpetuated lovingness through the practice of ho'oponopono in situations of density. Kupua principles address how harmony and balance can be achieved within (become pono again), and how higher consciousness is maintained when interacting in material density. The first seven principles are effectively stated in the Kupua teaching of Serge King. The first six tell you how to achieve the mechanics of being pono. The seventh is a summary of what you need to do (live) and how to evaluate if you really are living pono. Once you master the first seven, you are ready to move into the deeper mystical truths and advance spiritually using the eighth principle: The Power to Create Reality (*Ho'omanamana*) and operate the IAO process.

Operating Principles To Create Reality

Principle	**Knowledge**	**Transforming Reality Principle**
Ike	Awareness	The World Is What You Think It Is
Kala	Releasing	There Are No Limits
Makia	Focusing	Energy Flows Where Attention Goes
Manawa	Timing	Now Is The Moment Of Power
Aloha	Loving	Love Is To Be Happy With
Mana	Power Base	All Power Comes From Within
Pono	Right Action	Effectiveness is The Measure of Truth
Ho'omana	Reality	The Power To Create Realities

To put the principles to good use, each truth needs to be felt, not just intellectually processed, because the world responds to your thoughts. In fact, it is an exact mirror image of what you think and the beliefs you hold; it supports "who you are" (your consciousness) and what you want to create.

Operating Principles Defined

The Kahuna Kupua of old Hawaii developed the principles whereby the qualities of their spirituality expressed were consistently effective in their personal and professional lives. The secret to operating Kupua principles is defined by Serge King:

> "They have learned that the world quite naturally responds to their thoughts. It is, in effect, an exact

reflection of what they think it is, no more, and no less than a dream."

Additionally, the Kupua shaman knows that the dream called physical reality is generated from beliefs, expectations, intentions, fears, emotions, and inspired aspirations. Using the principles of consciousness awareness, you are creating and living your dream. Individually, each principle carries a great amount of mana. Collectively they form a powerful creative manifesting grid. Beliefs create fundamental standards and the rules to achieve and maintain them. There are eight major shamanic principles, which build the foundation to create reality out of realities in the concept of these five basic levels of reality:

Assumptions for Understanding Kupua Principles

- Everything is Alive (can be communicated with)
- Everything has Free Will
- Everything seeks Love
- Everything seeks Power
- Everything seeks Harmony

Transformative Shaman Principles Summary

1. IKE: Defines what it is
2. KALA: Clears the way to make it possible
3. MAKIA: Instructs you how to use it
4. MANAWA: Tells you when to use it
5. ALOHA: Identifies what the power is
6. MANA: Locates the source within
7. PONO: Action of aloha and result of using it
8. HO'OMANA: Makes it happen

1. Ike: The World Is What You Think It Is. Ike defines *what* it is. Ike contains the resources to see, know, feel, recognize, perceive, experience, understand, and to create. Ike is the Divine energy force used to manifest everything. The principle of Ike concludes that not only *can* you create anything you want, but also you *do* create everything in your life every day.

Be Aware. Your thoughts create everything. Everything manifests from Divine Energy. How you make it happen is by the thoughts you think and the actions you take. The meaning of your experience depends on your interpretation of it and/or your decision to accept someone else's interpretation. The decision to accept an assumption is also arbitrary. Thus, if the systems work for you, use them; if they don't, use something else. An effective shaman feels free to change systems at will, according to the situation at hand. This corollary also allows a great deal of tolerance for other systems because using a different reasoning isn't threatening. It is simply a different way to view life. Everything that we experience is interpreted according to our own BS (belief systems) and the reality in which we choose to function.

2. Kala: There are No limits. Kala *clears* the way. Kala means to loosen, release, take away, forgive, and to pardon. The meaning of kala is used in every level of reality. There is a formula to release, modify, change, integrate, expand, or create differently. Everything can be changed. Kala is the freedom to release what you don't want, modify or make changes to expand, improve or create what you do want.

Release to Set Free. The *releasing to set free action* effectively uncreates realities that no longer work and generates new possibilities. This imparts the freedom to change your mind about the limits you've set on health, happiness, prosperity, and the past, present, and future. Limits and limitations set for anything, useful or not, are all made up to structure the belief system in which you choose to function. This principle carries within it the belief that anything and everything is possible. The universe is infinite and we are all powerful and limitless beings of light. The individual is liberated to change mindsets and shift beliefs in order to achieve the best effects in any given situation.

3. Makia: Energy Flows Where Attention Goes. Makia *instructs* you how to use the awareness of your surroundings to manifest by concentration. Makia means to pin, bolt or nail. Mana is manifested via focused intent. Intent is a decision that directs awareness. Remember that energy flows where attention goes. Everything is energy: Thought is energy and energy patterns can be converted into others. You have ability to focus upon what is happening and follow it, or just as quickly affect a change of circumstances instantly.

Be Focused. To effectively use the makia principle takes concerted effort to focus only upon what you want, not on what you don't want. Your thoughts energize your behavior and your behavior energizes your thoughts. In using this formula, the individual commits to a *concentration of consciousness* connected with the object of focus. It is precisely the focused intent that commands action, whether physical or not. The energy thus concentrated will have a creative effect, according to the nature of the thoughts that accompany your attention.

4. Manawa: Now Is The Moment Of Power. Manawa tells you *when* to use it. *I keia manawa* means *Right Now*. The ancient ones believed that all time is now. Shamans activate and shift energy in the present moment. Empowerment happens in the now! What you do right now reshapes all past beliefs and activities. What you want, think, visualize, say, and do right now affects everything. Be aware of what influences are from the past. To be effective, remain centered completely in the present and focused on the most appropriate timing for events.

Be Centered Now. Be centered in the present when you want to be strong in holding the position or stay on course. Now is the time to influence events. The Kupua knowingly operates where the strongest point of power exists in the seat of emotions. Their sense of time is quite different from that of the typical person. They know that they cannot act in the past or the future, so they do not bring attention to the negative past. From this present moment, Kupua can influence both previous and potential events by using the appropriate date, time, or season.

5. Aloha: To Create Love – To Love Is To Be Happy With. Aloha *identifies* what the power is. Aloha *Is* the power. The Shaman uses the power of love in all actions. Love is the strongest force to create joy and happiness or break down barriers to forming pono.

Be Loving. One of the most profound and empowering discoveries is that love works better than anything else as a tool for effective action. For the Kupua, love or aloha is a spiritual and physical power that increases as judgment and criticism decrease. A truly loving intent is the most powerful spiritual force the world can know. The Kupua expresses aloha as a blessing, praise, appreciation, and gratitude. Separation diminishes power; love diminishes separation and therefore power increases. Love is the life force through which all share and evolve. It is the motivating factor underlying all of life. Expressing love and pleasure, or the lack thereof, is always very powerful. So be happy with what's good, and count your blessings to increase them. Love grows in gratitude and praise, caring touch, and joyful service. God *is* Love. God *is* Aloha. Aloha transforms chaos into harmony and balance.

6. Mana: All Power Comes From Within. Mana *locates* the source within. Mana comes from Hika-Po-Loa and is the power for miracles of healing, prophecy, interaction and illumination. It is the principle of Divine inner power. Shamans increase capacity to intake mana through spiritual expansion. All power integrates to serve others. You always have the mana you need to accomplish whatever you truly desire. As you feel harmony within yourself, you know you are attuned to the essence of Divine Love. You can discern untapped or hidden energy within your own Self and instinctively know where to find it.

Be Empowered. Mana is the result of being connected to Divine Source. If you are not confident, you are not connected. Mana must be built through studied intellectual, psychic, spiritual and physical discipline. The more you are in touch with the true essence of who you are, the more accessible your inner power becomes. Knowing the sixth principle, the Kupua functions from *Mana Pihi*, (supreme, absolute power). The Kupua has only to draw from Divine Source within to increase and use mana.

7. Pono: Effectiveness Is The Measure Of Truth. Pono is the *action* of aloha and the *result* of using it. In truth, pono is the result of using higher consciousness as a standard of conduct. Pono means good, righteous and proper. As a verb, it means to be; to be right or balanced. Mystically, the verb pono means to be blessed. We are blessed and we bless others. In this deeper context, it conveys the thought of personal and professional excellence with integrity. As a shaman tool, pono provides a way to know truth by observing behavior.

Be Blessed. Pono is the fruit of aloha action. Definitions of pono include: Goodness, uprightness, morality, correct procedure, and excellence. Choose thoughts and actions that create and bless the highest good. This principle calls us to be successful through *mana pono* – strength in purity, wellness, and integrity. When you do this, you attain an exquisite sense of satisfaction within your self and attain perfection in relationships. Being eminently practical in implementing higher consciousness, the Kupua perspective develops the principle that pono in daily life is a valid measure of your effectiveness to express lovingness and be in alignment to create harmony and balance. The pono person works to improve the conditions in the community, and to bless it as a whole, not for personal gain or glorification. Seek the *Way of Pono* – loving action.

8. Ho'omana: The Power to Create Reality. Ho'omana *makes it happen.* Ho'omana is the traditional Hawaiian theology. In practice, it is the means whereby to make reality of Divine Power. Actually, it is an integrating and a multiplying of both human and Divine mana (mana-mana). The Mystical properties of this old Hawaiian magic carry within it the IAO principle of Divine Energy, which gives birth to multiplicities. It is the ability to knowingly use any state of consciousness in multi-frameworks, and in doing so, it emanates from and is an integral part of Spirit essential to the completeness and oneness of its whole. It carries responsibility to use the power to create in the perfection of loving action, in multi-dimensions where inner and outer realities are fluid.

Make it Happen. Ho'o means to make it happen. Using *ho'ike* is to show, demonstrate, explain, reveal and experience. This creative philosophy of life is designed to aid in building a firm social, spiritual and moral foundation. If we consciously create life through higher consciousness intelligence, it provides cultivation of the skills and abilities to create and recreate our reality the way we envision our life to be. The secret of Ho'omana Kahiko lies in this Divine power of illumination, prophecy, and healing. The pattern was instilled in the first man, Kumuhonua, by Hika-Po-Loa. It continues to be treasured by those who intrinsically know the spiritual power of Ho'omana evidenced by building faith in life and in discerning the meaning of human existence. These qualities enable us to realize the fullness of our pono capabilities as higher consciousness beliefs are created and the Aka (ethereal link with the Gods) is strengthened.

Ho'omanamana Mystical Process

The Ho'omana is an expanded consciousness mystical process that evokes and works with all the raw elements of nature. Through the essence of rock and flames, of sea and winds, a mysterious fifth element can be accumulated. The principle of creating mana in the dynamics of Ho'omanamana (supernatural energy) is sometimes revered as healing and at other times perceived as miraculous phenomena. It functions from the code that you are a creator; there is nothing that you cannot change. This ability to create all things was often feared as sorcery because, although it may be used for doing great good in healing, there was fear that it could also cause evil. Sorcery, the ability to control natural forces through supernatural means, was often suspect for black arts. The truth is that it all depends upon the orientation of the thoughts and deeds of the practitioner. Hale Kuamoi Kikowaena warned:

> "There are shadow sides of ho'omanamana ... such as death prayers (*ana'ana*), making wind bodies (*kino makani*) ... causing spirit possession (*akua noho*), and using the poison gods (*kalai-pahoa*) and familiar spirits (*unihipili*)."

Ho'omana mystics stretch old and unused energy into patterns to convert to greater purpose. The practice transmits most powerfully through the I-A-O (creation point) of Hika-Po-Loa to make it happen (manifest) in the very best way possible. Briefly, these are the three aspects of the IAO process:

I (Ee): Connects the creative act with I'O
A (Ah): Ignites Divine flame to birth, nurture, and grow
O (Oh): Reveals, directs, and operates manifesting flow

The mystics comprehend ho'omanamana principles. Mysticism of the Hindu Upanishad describes the ho'omanamana realm:

> "There the eye goes not; speech goes not, nor the mind. We know not, we understand not how one would teach it."

Steps in Ho'omanamana Practice

1. Everything is a manifestation of Divine Energy. Amazing powers and capabilities are innate capabilities humans possess through the expanded consciousness process of Ho'omana.

2. Divine Energy is not self-existent nor is it self-created, but depends upon the mysterious source through Hika-Po-Loa symbolized by the name I-A-O. These are the creation points:

> **I** (eeh) is the creative act: that which is perfect manifests the creator (person), who is perfect, and can only create that which is perfect.
>
> **A** (ah) is the radiation of Divine Energy: as the universe of multi-dimensions.
>
> **O** (oh) is developing the ability to make reality of Divine Power so it can experience unreality as well.

3. The vital Power Contact may be established only through prayer and meditation.

4. Mana increases in direct proportion to one's physical, emotional, mental, and spiritual investment.

5. The capacity to use mana expands with dedication and practice. It develops in scope and power through establishing direct Power Contact with Hika-Po-Loa.

6. Selfless service brings joy in the beauty of nature to combine with mutual love.

Chapter 9. The Realities of The Kupua

"In philosophy, reality is the state of things as they actually exist, rather than as they may appear or might be imagined. Reality includes everything that is and has been, whether or not it is observable or comprehensible. A still broader definition includes that which has existed, exists, or will exist."

— *Wikipedia*

The desire to stand in harmony with reality is a most powerful motivation; it supports us to be the most responsible, loving human being we can be. Essentially, the Kupua lives in and experiences the same world as everyone else. He or she is using the same multi-dimensional mind whereby communications take place on many different levels, all at the same time. However, the Kupua consciously sees the world (and beyond) in the understanding of *'oia 'i'o* (the essence of truth) to be the fundamental nature of reality and in addition, chooses to function differently based on acquiring metaphysical knowledge of the eighth principle. While most people are unaware of the inner and outer dimensional dynamics of the world in which they live, the mystical Kupua embraces the practices of ho'omana to function within the expertise of the reality of each system framework.

The Kupua shamanic principles of reality is a system of knowledge that is about the mind and its effects on the world. It is a way of understanding and using the many frameworks of reality beliefs. In healing work, the shaman's view of reality is very different from the one most of society uses. The Kupua are healers between mind and body, between people, between people and circumstances, between humans and Nature, and between matter and Spirit. It is this viewpoint of realities, which really sets them apart from other healers.

The Kupua learns how to make physical and esoteric reality of Divine Power. Expanding into the mystical perception of the principles, which create reality, is the same natural skill every person has and effectively uses daily. It is so normal, that most people don't notice it at all. Ordinarily you do not face reality unless it is a reality you want to create. Think about it; any reality only exists because someone has focused it into being.

> "The mystic intuitively senses 'Reality' and instinctively knows 'The Truth.' A mystic is a person who has an inner sense of Life and Unity with the Whole."
> - Ernest Shurtleff Holmes
> *The Science of Mind*

The Kupua learns to function in all levels of consciousness and all systems and frameworks. Realities are viewed through a set of beliefs, assumptions, attitudes, and expectations. Each reality is a rich environment, which enables the Kupua to function in the appropriate physical, metaphysical, symbolic, oneness, or dream world formula that is the most empowering.

One reality is not more advanced than another; just more convenient or more appropriate for completing certain tasks. Consider the ranges of consciousness in which to function in both night and day activities. Part of the time the conscious mind is asleep, yet consciousness keeps working 24 hours a day to support the endless creating of realities your mind generates. The flexibility of mystical thinking brings awareness that there are many choices of realities that provide numerous ways to think and act.

Ho'omanamana Reality – Creating Realities

Ho'omanamana is concentrated thought power from which all is manifested. Manamana means to impart extraordinary mana and is a means to transcend beyond human limitations. The first consideration is in expansion of our scope of thought, as well as the need to increase and strengthen our spirituality, self-assurance and knowledge at all levels. Operating in the levels of reality are all useful tools in understanding the basic approaches to existence and the operating principles used to express mana effectively. To understand it, think about the root meaning of Ho'o, which means to cause or create. Leinani Melville's *Esoteric Hawaiian Dictionary* defines it this way:

1. To cause a thing to happen, bring about an effect; produce a result, advocate and produce a consequence.

2. To reach, extend, and stretch, to reach into one's mind for a thing by exerting one's will in order to recall an incident.

3. To communicate with or get in touch with someone, project one's thought to another who is either nearby or distant, use transference of thought called "the coconut wireless system."

4. To transcend human limitations, reach with one's mind into the Spirit World; extend one's psychical powers into the supernatural; extend the invisible spiritual communication cord between finite man and infinite God via the medium of prayer.

5. To get into one's inner mind by the power of positive thought, to extend one's thought into the inner Kingdom of God with ho'omanamana by means of silent meditation (concentrated thought power).

Ho'omanamana expertise contributes to increased confidence as environments of each reality expression become familiar.

Reality Divisions

The reality divisions illustrate Hawaiian and English words, which represent major reality categories, framework focus, and express experiences differently. The location of the framework describes the boundary/freedom of the belief, which is to be expressed. The five reality divisions are summarized below:

Reality Divisions Chart

Reality Levels	Reality	Framework	Experience
1. Ike Papakahi	Physical	Separate	Scientific
2. Ike Papalua	Psychic	Connected	Metaphysical
3. Ike Papakolu	Symbolic	Meaning	Significance
4. Ike Papaha	Oneness	Being	Unity, Merge
5. Ike Papalima	Dream	Consciousness	Dimensions

Different belief systems generally fall into five major reality categories, which produce their own set of rules relating to the unique purposes that are universal and specific to that reality. This summary gives you an idea of each framework:

The Five Major Levels of Reality

1. Physical: Physical laws set scientific reality
   All people, places, and things are separate
   We experience in physically separate ways
   Physical action affects change in other realities

2. Psychic: Psychic laws set subjective reality
   All people, places, and things are energy
   Mental and emotional energy laws govern
   All people, places, and things are connected
   All people, places, and things can communicate
   We converse through a telepathic principle
   Consciousness can be transferred
   Metaphysical action affects other realities

3. Symbolic: All people, places, and things have meaning
   Symbolism holds consciousness
   Symbols are used as vehicles of communication
   Meaning is conveyed through symbolism

     Symbols affect people, places, and things
     Symbolism affects other realities

4. Oneness: Oneness is all there is
     We are One
     We merge into one consciousness
     We merge with other people, places, and things
     Oneness is an abstraction
     Oneness affects other realities

5. Dream: All of life is a dream
     We dream life into PEMS realities
     Night dream function reflects waking activity
     Day dream function reflects night activity
     Dream reality carries ho'omanamana
     All levels of consciousness are used in dreaming
     Dreaming affects other realities

Shaman Realities Defined

1. Ike Papakahi – Physical Reality: It is the Objective World, which functions within the framework that everything is separate. The experience is scientific. The implementation tools are Linear Physical Expertise in duality. We seek individual permanence.

2. Ike Papalua – Psychic Reality: It is the Subjective World, which functions within a metaphysical framework that everything is connected. The experience is psychically expressed. The implementation tools are Intuitive Perceptions. We seek connectedness.

3. Ike Papakolu – Symbolic Reality: It is the Representative World, which functions within the framework that everything has meaning. The experience is significance expression. The tool of implementation is Appreciation. We seek value.

4. Ike Papaha – Oneness Reality: It is the Holistic World, which functions within the framework that everything is Beingness. Experience is unity expressed. The implementation tool is merging into Beingness. We seek immortality.

5. Ike Papalima – Dream Reality: It is the Dream World, which functions in all frameworks to create reality 24 hours a day (asleep or awake), where everything is imaginative. Dreaming takes place in our minds before it is sent to one of the levels of reality to carry out action. The experience is one of weaving reality into multidimensional expression. These magical elements are also used during *moe uhane* – nighttime dreaming, in Dreams of the Spirit, lucid or in conscious application. We seek dimensional expression.

> "And spirit continues to create physical forms, and conditions for its human experiences, and that through human experiences the mind of man easily loses 'reality' by disconnecting itself from spirit and spirit realities."
> - Mahealani Kuamoo'o-Henery

Moving Between Realities

All people shift mindsets (move between realities) as a natural process instinctively. However, the Kupua Shaman learns to shift mindsets in full conscious selection. The main obstacle for the untrained is the interference of critical analysis that impinges from a different reality system. For example: It is quite natural to practice telepathy when you are in the belief system of the second level of reality (psychic). However, operating in the psychic level of reality, where everyone and everything is psychic, if you hold strongly to the beliefs of the physical reality, you would carry the conviction that you are not psychic. When you tell yourself that you are not psychic, you create the illusion to yourself that you are not psychic. Additionally, using the tool of visualization to gain the skill will do you little good if you keep saying to yourself, "I am not clairvoyant."

Weaving in and out of realities is normal and happens automatically as you begin to be inspired to view or experience things from a different perspective. The beliefs of one mindset are easily modified and/or changed because you can literally move into a different belief system. In fact, in order to move easily and effectively between realities, you must be willing to leave each mindset as you move to the next (or learn to function in both realities combined).

Kahea (changing reality) is done through the shifting of emotional-intellectual mana flow. Reality is called into being. This is why healing by chants (*La'au Kahea*) and hula is used to embody the Divine to create a different reality. The major mana used in changing realities flows through empowered aka lines. Shamans move between different realities to use the perspective that works the best for the task at hand, and to help people who prefer to function in different reality beliefs. Moving between realities is easily accomplished using dream weaving through the use of inspiration and imagination. This allows you to function in any reality and also use information from one mode for use in any other.

The following exercise is rewarding and fun! This is how it works:

- Start by thinking about moving clouds. Observe or just imagine clouds. Let your imagination slip into the levels of reality, which is a vast playground waiting to be explored. In the 1st level, the cloud is viewed from a physical image. You will describe many of its physical features: the visual shape, color or the scientific properties. After a while you will automatically move through the levels of reality as your natural, curious, inquiring mind observes.

- In the 2nd level, it is natural to turn your observation into listening from your heart. You begin to quite naturally communicate with the cloud. It may speak to you during changing images or communicate through telepathic impressions. Different shapes begin to convey meaning as you slip into the wonderment of the shifting panorama.

- In the 3rd level, the cloud is a symbolic canvas adopting different forms in your imagination that convey meaning. Pictures are easy to discern and tap into energy patterns embedded in the clouds. As your awareness increases, the magic and mystery begin to permeate your senses.

- In the 4th level of oneness, you become the cloud. When focus is moved from viewing or communicating into being, you shapeshift. You become an integral part of the cloud in oneness. You think as it thinks, feel, and act as if you are the actual cloud itself (not as an observer). You merge into the consciousness of the cloud and it merges into your consciousness where the dream reality flourishes.

- In the 5th level, you dream the cloud (imagine it) in fluidity and flexibility creating ho'omana realization. Reality becomes as dimensional as you want it to be. You dream with the cloud. This is called dream weaving. Notice how you dream up thoughts or pictures from the dream state part of your mind, where it germinates before you begin to function in the physical or other reality frameworks.

Ultimately, the perception of reality is what you think it is. As a society, we are constantly blending our sense of realism. We create a new world every day. Having crossed profound boundaries, we form a new context in which there is an urge to deal with the reality of our world as it is presently seen and as it is becoming. The core challenge of our times is transforming our culture to fit our sense of new realities. Kahu Hale Makua felt strongly that the time has come to establish a comprehensive and universal understanding about the nature of reality and our own nature. Our holistic (pono), mental-emotional, and physical perspective fosters the growth of our spiritual consciousness through multilevel realities. Kahu Hale said:

> "A new synthesis, a conjoining of the tangible and intangible levels of reality that bring science and spirituality together, enables an extension of our senses and allows us to access the hidden vocabulary that lie behind the veil of ignorance and matter."

Chapter 10. Mysteries of Mana

The mysteries of mana (life force) flow through all of life. Mana is defined by Puki & Elbert as: Supernatural or Divine power and authority. It translates to mean *power*. However, the concept of power does not equate to material possessions or symbols of wealth and status. Herb Kawainui Kane, Hawaiian author and artist-historian depicts Mana in these terms:

> "*Mana* was the force that powered the universe - expressed in everything from the movements of the stars to the growth of a plant or the surge of a wave. Human *mana* - manifested as life force, charisma, inherited talents, intelligence, and other virtues – flowed down the same hereditary channel of seniority from the major spirits (*akua*) to the ancestral spirits (*'aumakua*) to living parents (*makua*) and their children. The inheritance of certain talents within a family was taken as evidence of mana being passed down the line of seniority."

Mana of an individual, place or thing is an all-encompassing electro-vital consciousness force, greater than energy alone. It is the essence of life itself and the basis of all thought processes and bodily function. There are two types of mana: the mana you are born with and the mana gained throughout life. An example can be seen in the late Hawaiian Senator Daniel K. Inouye's life and career. He demonstrated inherited personal mana and professional mana gained from the position he held as the second longest-serving senator in U.S. history. The beloved Inouye was often described as "soft spoken, modest, and a man of integrity." His last word was aloha, which holds the highest expression of mana.

The Ancient Empowerment Practice

> "Mana is the single most important gift you may receive from the Gods, and you will receive it... if... you participate fully in the rites and practices of Ho'omana Kahiko."
>
> - Kahu Lanakilahuokalani Brandt

The ancient empowerment practice is called Ho'omana Kahiko. Ho means to cause, 'O is the resources for creating, and Mana indicates the power, life force energy on every level. Thus, Ho'omana means to cause the process of creating empowerment. It entailed establishing direct Power Contact through continuous nourishing mana with prayer and meditation. The esoteric term mana'o means empowerment within one's own mind or thought. It is the lower physical consciousness of the human brain, which powers the conscious mind. Melville's *Esoteric Hawaiian Dictionary*(78)defines mana'o as an empowerment practice, which means:

1. Of the mind.
2. Mind power; power of the mind, power of thought, power of thinking.
3. To think, conceive; reflect upon a subject, to determine by thinking; to think one's way through a problem, to think one's way out of a situation; to make a decision; to reach a conclusion.
4. To realize; realization, to imagine.
5. To exercise one's power of judgment, to judge in accordance with one's way of thinking.
6. To will; wish.
7. To desire; crave, yearn, as long for appeasement of one's carnal appetite or crave for the satisfying of one's material desires; an expression of desire.

Mana 'o i'o means the higher mind of the soul. It is the thought power of the inner (soul) consciousness of the inner spiritual being, your real spiritual self, which takes residence within the human body to learn lessons from earthly experiences.

Gathering Mana

Gathering mana is a natural flow of life force generated through pono (balanced actions). Meditation and disciplines enhance the gathering of mana flow, but it takes living in harmony with yourself, those around you, environment and the Divine to gather an abundance of mana. In the book *Fundamentals of Hawaiian Mysticism*, Charlotte Berney explains that gathering mana is the very act of having meaningful work to do, it is enjoying harmonious relationships with those around you, and being of service to others in some way.

Every creature has the required amount of Mana to maintain his or her minimal, natural spiritual, psychic and physical patterns. Gathering an abundance of mana is the power to do anything that you decide to do. To fully practice Ho'omana (charging your batteries), you must invest time to recharge your psychic and spiritual batteries in sincere prayer-communication with your Aumakua, Hika-Po-Loa, and with those Divine contacts dictated by your priestly or lay vocation. Kahu Brandt puts it this way:

> "Because Mana absolutely cannot be acquired by wishing or hoping, osmosis or inept prayers; it must be built through studied intellectual, psychic, spiritual and physical disciplines."

According to Keoni Pilipa'a in *Mindfulness in Stone Age Hawaii, What the Old Kahunas Knew...*, gathering personal mana was a spiritual practice of the Kahuna, *ali'i* (royalty), heroes, warriors, and other practitioners who were able to collect mana-ali'i (chiefly power). This came from meticulously obeying the rules of taboo (most sacred), *mana-ola* (life giving power), which certain specialists could possess, and *manakua* (absolute and everlasting power of the gods). He said that this was the mana from the other side of this mana and is the squared equation explained in Ho'omanamana, "...held within the hands of I'O, the Supreme Being."

Priests collected mana by performing rituals that utilized specific actions taken while *"maintaining the 'aha"* (the thread of awakened consciousness). Aha is the invisible spiritual channel through which we breathe, as the organs connected with the lungs. The invisible channel links the finite mind of humanity with the Universal Mind of God. *Ahu* refers to the action of the charging of the batteries that generates, regenerates and transforms power.

Movement of Mana

It is important to know not only what mana is, but also how it is utilized. Mana is higher consciousness collected in pockets throughout PEMS (physical, emotional, mental, and spiritual) bodies. The flow radiates through the layers and develops into mana strands (threads) of aka chords. The transmission of mana is a means to focus, communicate, and eventually convey the subtler forms of energy. These are filtered through sensory input, guiding physical actions, empathizing with others, and are the life-force consciousness transmission of all internal and external receptors. Mana is received and distributed through the Senses, Will, and Imagination.

Senses: Mana is transmitted by impulses through your senses, feelings, and the innate radiance of your being. It affects you and others, with or without your knowledge.

Will: Mana transmits in thought fed in flashes of perception. Will selects from your choice of consciousness levels, which determine and direct your attention, emotion, and meaning.

Imagination: Imagination (the Imago) is a manifestation of the force of Spirit. Mana flows through imagination in pictures and words. Words also create and rearrange energy patterns. Passion and emotions shift levels of consciousness that bring influence and dynamics. Your stockpile of imagination is drawn from past, present and future events through choices about how you perceive them. Your reality is imagined to fit your beliefs about yourself, others, and events. As your beliefs change, your images and vocabulary also change. Old ways, traditions and dogmas that no longer work are released to make way for a newer and greater perception of spiritual purpose. When you hold on to past beliefs, you continue to function from the limited view, knowledge, maturity, and comprehension you held at the time of the original experience. Each review of any incident offers the choice to experience it in the same, lower or higher consciousness expression.

How Does Mana Flow?

Mana flows within you through your thoughts, beliefs, and actions. All flow conveys the level of consciousness expressing the quality of mana you are able to create, store, and maintain to use in daily life, and in service to others. Principles describe higher consciousness guidelines, which provide the capacity to utilize greater amounts of mana as the initiate advances in spiritual development. The ability to receive greater amounts of mana flow depends upon developing higher levels of consciousness practices. Knowing how these components work together is the formula to how seeming miracles of healing and transformation are created. How you do this directly impacts others with the power of loving mana.

The mana of the Triune Selves depicts the flowing relationship of the layers of higher consciousness within yourselves as it attains the relationship of lokahi. Lokahi is the foundation upon which to communicate and illuminate healing. In this higher state of oneness, lokahi is a way of focusing and gathering energy into one point for the purpose of reconstructing the Mind, Body and Spirit. The method of healing (*'ike Haha*) taught by Kahuna Kalua Kaiahua of Maui, removes blockages and restores circulation. This integration of the very highest Spirit supports you to live in loving alignment and with the flow of healing (*ho'ola*) mana. Thus, your ability to generate and maintain mana develops with your dedication to living lovingness. When you say, "No to doing the *Density Dance*," say,

"Yes, to function in the flow of Mana," and choose a worthy and exciting purpose, your *"Greater Purpose"* will be fulfilled.

Mana flows automatically among all people, places, and things. The spiritual strength and power of mana is present everywhere. You have only to look to nature to observe the flow. Ocean waves have mana. Fish have mana. There are places that relax, restore, revitalize, and heal through the flow of mana. When you enter these natural places of nature or those that are maintained by the ancestors, you may feel their presence, which will cause you to notice a sense of sacredness, wonder, awe, peace or calm. These are commonly known as vortexes, where you are able to access mana by being there.

The heiau (temples) are containers of mana flow because they are places where people worship traditional Hawaiian akua (gods) and aumakua (family gods). People give pule (prayers), mele (chants) and ho'okupu (offerings), which strengthen the presence of the akua in the temple, and the mana of those who offer them. The mana flow generated in the heiau help to reinforce the mana flow relationship of people to their gods and the connections with each other. Because the gods are manifested as nature, it supports humanity's link to the environment. As people offer pule and mele at heiau, the wisdom and knowledge in the words carry mana in the memory and instill the energy of the gods. The Hawaiian heiau provides a sacred space for the strengthening and flow of mana.

The flow of mana through all things is enhanced by a conscious choice to interact in the highest consciousness. Getting to know how your personal mana flow processing works starts with using the conscious mind. It is the first layer of rudimentary mana skills, which begin by using energy on the physical level through the ego, self-esteem, and other superficial power generating means. At some point, you discover more empowering levels of the mind within your selves to gain the deeper access to the greatest mana flow for manifesting life.

Mana Flow Rules – The Kanawai Akua

Rules established for generating mana, maintaining a supply and ensuring flow from Hika-P0-Loa, are called Kanawai Akua. These are four basic rules taught by Kahu Brandt:

1. Live the Spirit of Aloha. This is a commitment to live and practice the Spirit of Aloha.
    a. Respect the rights and convictions of others
    b. Respect the person, properties, and prerogatives

2. Expand Your Powers. This enables you to be better suited to accept responsibilities as a Ho'omana (creator of empowerment) practitioner.
    a. Study both spiritual and material knowledge extensively
    b. Strive constantly to expand physical, emotional, intellectual knowledge, psychic, and spiritual powers

3. Fill Your Reservoir with Ike. This is Divine knowledge based on spiritual authority generated through the daily practice of Pule Ho'omana (prayer for empowerment). This prayer creates empowerment from:
    a. God – Hika-Po-Loa (Triumvirate Kane, Ku, and Lono)
    b. Your own Aumakua

4. Protect the Sanctity. Nurture your Ike and your Mana. Only you can protect the sanctity of your Ike and your Mana through the purity of your own life. Build the magic of Laau Kahea in the dynamism of its mana practices and scorn the work of the Kahuna Ana'ana. Apply these rules:
    a. Honor your God daily
    b. Nurture your Ike and your Mana in its highest form
    c. Avoid giving any of your power to greed or materialism
    d. Don't do black magic that brings evil to others

> "Always hold the greatest thoughts about anyone, anything or anyplace, especially towards yourself. For the natural rule is, if any, that YOU will always be the recipient."
>
> - Kahu Abraham Kawaii

Chapter 11. Maintain Mana Flow

We've discussed what mana is, how it works, the rules to generate mana and where it resides within your Triune Self. We have not covered how the flow of mana works consistently for the ordinary person and for the practitioner. Mana flow is always available. There is never down time where your mana is concerned. Maintaining mana flow relies upon your connection with your God. So be mindful of what you do and how you do it.

Mana Flow Decisions

The key to maintain mana flow (your life force) is first and foremost through the thinking behind your decisions. The thoughts you think and your attitudes (emotions) create your own reality about what you believe is and is not humanly possible for you. How confident you feel about how successful you are to execute what you think success should be is the amount of mana current that flows through your physical, emotional, mental and spiritual aka lines. The amount of mana flow you access is a moment-by-moment decision as to quantity you really want to use for your present situation. Your decision to function in a lower or higher consciousness determines how much mana you have available. Any disruption in mana flow is a decision made by you to not be in pono for some reason.

Sprinkled throughout the book are ways in which you can generate and maintain mana. However, techniques are just techniques. The truth is that every heart's impulse and desire is created every moment by your decisions to function in a lower or higher level of consciousness, and by every word you speak. Before you use any technique to create a new specific desire, think about what you have already created. Then ask yourself, "Is my new desire compatible with the desires I have already created or have set into motion?" In order to activate a new wish or goal successfully, you must be willing to give up your past beliefs. One way to do this is to understand what or why you created the past. You must be willing to change what does not support your present or new goal. You can decide if you want to continue to function in the environment that you are creating or take steps to change.

PEMS (physical, emotional, mental and spiritual) expressions are access channels in which mana flows. When channels are open, mana flows freely. If you block the channels for any length of time, flow stops. Thus, your primary test as a human is to be pono (in loving alignment). Getting out of density is not as easy as getting in because mana slows down when you choose density consciousness momentarily, or stops all together when you continue to express non-pono behavior. Your density choices result in your inability to achieve higher consciousness or function in pono. It is the fertile ground for the tool of denial. If you are functioning in pono'ole (*without pono*) some of these symptoms appear when you:

- Do not recognize the problem
- Intensely feel your pain, or the pain of others
- May try to hide it, but your focus becomes about you
- Your fears and personal survival become worrisome

It is natural to experience drama and trauma in density. You have established a density playing field where your addiction to getting your own way (at any cost) sets up a power and dominance game that you may not be able to easily resist. When you don't act in your natural loving nature (pono), you create an opportunity to test yourself or others. Recognize when you are choosing to be in density or in pono, and notice how that feels. It's important to know if you are on the right track, or if you need to focus more on aloha/pono development. Viewing specific conduct will help you recognize your behavior as pono action or pono'ole.

PEMS Mana Disruption Locater

When you play the density game in lower consciousness, your mana flow is disrupted. Serge King uses a disruptive code name as an identifying tool. The disruptive code name is an acronym created by using four descriptions, which clog your PEMS and wreak havoc with your life. Make up your own acronyms or use these responses to identify the emotional behavior that is required to function in density. These codes help you identify when you are not connected to Source and show when you are functioning in density:

- FUDS: Fear, Unhappiness, Doubt, or Stress
- BLOC: Blocked, Limitation, Obsession, or Confusion
- CRAP: Criticism, Resentment, Apathy, or Powerlessness
- DUMB: Dense, Unaware, Mindless, or Bored
- RAGS: Resentment, Anger, Guilt, or Strife
- HATE: Hinder, Abhor, Terrify, or Explode

Clear Disruptive Codes:

Techniques, exercises and therapeutic applications exist to clear clogged PEMS channels when you remain in density. Practice fundamental principles, and processes to increase and improve your pono skills. When any disruption occurs, do something to disconnect from the density and reconnect to your Higher Self to restore balance and activate your pono capability.

Barometer Charts indicate your high mana levels, point to your pono behavior, and show you where you are lured into density to demonstrate very little or no pono actions. Use these charts:

Mana Flow Indicator	Pono Behavior Rating
A. Full Mana Flow Capacity	Pono actions: Apparent
B. Mana Flow Fluctuating	Pono actions: Declining
C. Mana Flow Diverted	Pono actions: None

Pono: Highest Mana Flow Directed Barometer Chart

PEMS - Physical, Emotional, Mental, Spiritual Channel Access
<u>Assess: Do You Act in Pono or Not?</u>

HIGHER SELF CONSCIOUSNESS
Becoming the mystical shaman
Love, light, bliss, joy, peace
Passionate in doing things

OPTIMUM MANA FLOW
Enlightenment/higher self
Acceptance, reason, bless
Takes responsibility

MANA FLOWS AS REQUIRED
Full Mana flow capacity
Mental/emotional cooperation
Highest Divine connection
Three selves integrated
PEMS harmony and balanced
Confidence comes from within
Aloha, mana, pono alignment
Integrated spirit/mind/body

100% MANA FLOW
Pono operating
Integrates mana
Positive natural flow
Higher self function
Fulfilling life purpose
Reaches potential
Emanates caring
Humanity focus

1. Spiritual – Mystical
Uses highest consciousness
Haipule practices
Golden rule practices: Love

Integrate PEMS
Ho'ohuna alignment
Serves humanity
Spontaneous healing

2. Mental – Thinking
Rational thought
Good mental health
Enlightened mind

Express Higher Self
Forms ho'oponopono
Expansive perspective
Positive life outlook

3. Emotions – Feelings
Emotional maturity
Expresses love to self/others
Healing/ho'ola

Express Higher Self
Harmony and balance
Healthy personality
Happiness, joyful service

4. Physical – Strong Body
Maintains healthy body
Loving right action
Strength and endurance

Express Higher Self
No density – no disconnect
Satisfactory lifestyle
Friendship, stewardship

Pono Behavior is Possible Using Full Mana Flow

Review Pono Behavior Rating: Apparent

B. Pono Challenged: Moderate Mana Flow Barometer Chart

PEMS: Physical Emotional Mental Spiritual Channel Fluctuates
<u>*Assess: Do You Act in Pono or Not*</u>?

HIGHER AND LOWER SELF
Overcoming challenges
Desires to achieve good generally
Courage, neutrality, willingness
Emotion, mental, spiritual growth

LEARNING MANA FLOW
Testing pono standards
Learning mana skills
Developing coping skills
Acquiring service skills

MANA NEED FREQUENT REFILL
Mana flow fluctuating
Three selves often separated

% MANA FLOW FLUCTUATES
Spirituality entices
Positive/negative challenges

PEMS Mana Flow Strain
Moderate/ sporadic connection
PEMS balance/ imbalance

PEMS Harmony
Needs Ho'oponopono
Questions life's purpose

1. SPIRITUAL: MANA REDUCE
Spiritual Now Mental Based
Consciousness growth issues
Mana reduce: anger, bitterness
Strives for pono, aloha: harmony
Spirit/mind/body short-circuit

DENSITY KICKS IN
Internal Discord
Density entices
Haipule needed
Self-centered action
Seeks mana outside of self

2. MENTAL: BELIEF CHANGES
Mental Now Emotional Based
Rational thought diminishes
May doubt decision making
Can't always control thoughts
Use of mana vs. power
Struggles to find purpose

ACTIVATE DENSITY
Balances Power
Power/ dominance/ victim
Second guesses self
Racing thoughts
Not enough time
Loss of loving right action

PONO DESTRUCTIVE DENSITY CODES INSTALLED

<u>Emotional Reactions Serving In Density</u>
FUDS: Fear, Unhappiness, Doubt, or Stress
BLOC: Blocks, Limitation, Obsession, or Confusion
CRAP: Criticism, Resentment, Apathy, or Powerlessness
DUMB: Dense, Unaware, Mindless, or Bored

Illness Develops in Density

Review Pono Behavior Rating: Declining

C. Pono Flow: Low to No Mana Flow Barometer Chart

PEMS: Physical Emotional Mental Spiritual Channel Closed
<u>*Assess: Do You Act in Pono or Not?*</u>

LOWER CONSCIOUSNESS
Density: emotional reactions
Shame, guilt, apathy, grief, fear

MANA FLOW INDICATOR
Mana flow Diverted
Self-disconnect with three selves

PEMS Mana Drained
Irregular Divine connection
Procrastinates in doing things

3. EMOTIONAL: NO MANA FLOW
Emotional – Negative in Charge
Confidence – from outside stimuli
Need conflict resolution help
Megalomania grandeur delusions

Emotional Mana Loss Stages:
a. **Density**: Controls playing field
   Unpleasant, worry, sad, jealous
b. **Drama**: Stress, conflict:
   Dominant, subservient
c. **Victimhood**: Many issues
   Constant tragic episodes

4. PHYSICAL: NO MANA FLOW
Mana flow Disconnect
Internal/external health decline
Obsessive over health concerns
Frequent serious health crises

FULL BLOWN DENSITY
Challenge to grow
Vanity, desire, anger, pride

NO % MANA FLOW
Negative natural flow
Develop no coping skills

PEMS Disharmony
Density pervades
Lack of responsibility

DENSITY CONTROLS
Rogue Ego Conscious
Disruption codes intensify
Mental illness develops
Nervous breakdown

Density Powers PEMS
Negative Emotions
Discomfort, discouragement
Detrimental attitudes
Divisive behavior
Destructive emotions
No over-all life satisfaction

DENSITY OPERATES
Density PEMS Dis-ease
Serious illness develops
No self-control
Physical death results

PONO DESTRUCTIVE DENSITY CODES OPERATING

<u>Emotional Reactions Serving In Density</u>
RAGS: Resentment, Anger, Guilt, or Strife
HATE: Hinders, Abhors, Terrifies, or Explodes

Illness Intensifies Every Moment in Density

Review Pono Behavior Rating: None

Review Pono and Pono'ole Behavior

Review pono and pono'ole descriptions in the Barometer Charts on the prior three pages. Find your PEMS (*Physical Emotional Mental Spiritual*) quotient on the charts. You function differently depending on your emotional, intellectual, physical or spiritual dynamics in any action or response. Get into your exploration mode. Review and assess your pono and pono'ole responses and behaviors. Be as objective as possible from these evaluation categories:

- Loving pono behavior
- Pono activity decline
- Mostly density, non-loving behavior

Notice these points when evaluating your measure of pono:

- Confront positive and negative actions
- Notice signs of racing thoughts (you pass through racing thoughts just before reaching the emotional state)
- Check to see if you have any illness symptoms
- Discover if you have allowed fear to grip you
- Look to see what it is you fear
- Be honest with yourself
- Get to the root cause of your triggers
- Acknowledge if you have lost pono
- Decide what to do about it

Reconnect to Source

When you are not connected to Source, you do not have the capability at this time, no matter how advanced spiritually you have become, to function as a spiritually empowered Shaman or a respected Kahuna. Recognize when you are not connected to Divine Source. Higher Consciousness is a moment-by-moment decision, which you can easily lose if you develop habits of using the tools of density to gain a sense of power or prestige. When you are disconnected from your Source, techniques will not work effectively unless they help you to reconnect to the power within. It is vital that you take steps to change the condition that brought about the problem in the first place. All effective processes demand that you reconnect to your Source. In order to do this you might want to clear the HATE, cut the CRAP or clear any DUMB disruptive energy codes to be reconnected. Mana is activated by simple, everyday activities. If you are functioning in density and you want to get out of it, take steps to restore your mana connection immediately.

This is a quick method to reconnect to Source. You must immediately focus all your attention on a different task. This works because a different awareness automatically creates a change in mana flow. Use these short steps:

- Concentrate fully on a different task for 5 minutes
- Be totally engulfed within yourself and the activity
- Enjoy what you are doing for its own sake

The key is to focus upon what you really enjoy doing. The result of your new focal point is that mana surfaces of its own accord. Your will comes from a program already formed. Turn it on further with an impassioned imagination. When you follow this short mana restoration formula, the grip of density is suspended. You have to put the trauma and drama out of your mind for an instant and focus upon something else. This action restores your natural mana flow state and then, in a state of harmony and balance, you can proceed with other activities to address the condition that sent you off track.

One of the most powerful methods that fills your physical, emotional, and mental body to manifest your heart's desire has all the essentials of connecting to the Divine on all levels and balances all major energies flowing on Earth. Called Kalana Hula Meditation, it integrates a variety of modalities within the practice. Inside the powerful manifesting tool are several mana-enhancing methods: HA Breath, Haipule, and Ha'a/Hula movement. To activate mana flow, follow the simple instructions to experience a wonderful shamanic practice I learned from Kahu Serge and Kumu Susan.

Kalana Hula Manifesting Meditation Practice

1.) **Connect with Aumakua – Piko Piko Meditation:** Use HA Breath to Empower the highest connection or simply breathe as you connect to your mana flow. Piko Piko meditation means using Ha Breath to connect Source and center-to-center.

Begin with Kala – Intention and Clearing: Use Piko Piko to cleanse and align your Bowl of Light centers (crown, navel, genitals) or on the inhale think: *God, Divine Presence, I'O, or Mana.* On the exhale think, *Release or I am.* Do not throw energy; just think different aspects. Energy automatically goes where you think, exchanges mana, and naturally balances. Feel yourself in alignment as you repeat centering with each mana flow choice. Additional centering ideas are shown below:

Preparation and Centering Guide

Intake	Exhale	Akua	Aspects of Self
Heaven	Earth	Kane	Aumakua, Higher Self
Earth	Crown	Lono	Conscious Mind
Crown	Navel	Ku	Subconscious Mind
Navel	World	Kanaloa	Integrate God Self-Mana

2.) **Set Intention:** Form a Wish Globe in which to create your desire (connect the tip of your thumbs and fingers around the navel). Make a brief statement of what you want to create. Continue holding the globe positioned for your desire at your navel until the process is completed. Note: Mana builds as you focus on your desire.

3.) **Invoke Mana through the Elements of Nature:** We call in each Element one by one. Nalu (ponder it) or channel it. Breathe in: Allow each Element to fill you as you beckon each one. Feel the empowerment of Divine energy with each intake. As the elements flood into you, be empowered by the Hawaiian phrase "*Ho'opaipai O Ke Nalu.*" This means to encourage, rouse, stir, excite. The reference is to surfing - It means to call in the perfect wave. Spiritually, it is a proclamation commanding the energy of each element to join your will. Release each Element with the thought, *Mahalo* (thank you).

Elements of Nature: The Elements of Nature are: Fire, Air, Water, Earth, Plant, Animal, People, and Spirit. Call each one separately to permeate your Wish Globe. As you beckon the elements of Nature, say or think the Hawaiian and English words. Notice what form each element presents itself to flow through you. Notice the consciousness, what the element does, and the purpose of the empowerments.

Elements of Nature Chart

Hawaiian	English	What it Does – Purpose
Ahi	Sun/Fire	Burn out, release, transform
Makani	Wind/Air	Give life, free forces, change
Wai	Water	Nurture, restore mana
Pohaku	Stone/Earth	Rebuild strength, stabilize
La'au	Plant	Root the mana, growth
Holoholona	Animal	Life, will, promote mobility
Kanaka	People	Blessing, integrate lovingness
I'O, IAO	Spirit	Permeating God relationship

4.) **Invoke Powers of the IAO Principles**: IAO Chant:

EEE... AAA... AAAH... OOO... OOH...
(Repeat chant seven times.)

5.) **Call Blessing with the Au'makua Prayer:**
(Repeat prayer three times)

Au'makua, mai ka po wai ola, ho'ikea mai I ke ola

Higher Self, bring forth the water of life from out of the realm of Spirit and manifest these blessings.

6.) **Haipule Intention:** Bless in energy and words. Imagine and visualize the desired action. After completion, cup Wish Globe in your hands. Move it from Navel to position in front of your face. Gently release your hands to send the wish off with a blessing. Blow as a kiss as you release your hands skyward. Feel the sacredness and blessing.

7.) **Closing Action:** Put your left foot forward as you extend your left arm with fist facing downward. Strike left hand with right palm (opening left palm) while shouting, **"Pau!"** (It is finished!).

8.) **Closing declaration: Amama, ua noa!** (So be it. It is done!)

Although mana is a spiritual substance that is carried in the molecules of everything, and it may be likened to the soft breeze of breath, its symbol is water. So the flow of mana is like a current of water. Other mana flow descriptions are made by Kenneth Meadows in *Shamanic Spirit: A Practical Guide to Personal Fulfillment*:

> "Mana, then, is not a physical energy but a spiritual essence with a fluidity, which likens it to electricity and, like an electric current, its flow is at different strengths or voltages.
>
> At a basic level it keeps the physical and energetic bodies functioning.
>
> At a higher frequency it is the vitality that enables you to *think*.
>
> At a higher strength still, it is a power that restores to wholeness in all dimensions, for it is the power of healing or *whole*-ness.
>
> Mana at its different 'strengths' thus enables all the 'bodies' that comprise our total being to function efficiently. The finer and more subtle the 'body' the stronger must be the Mana to power it.
>
> Mana has been likened to fine rain, which causes shoots to burst forth from seed and grow into plants and trees and bear fruit – for Mana saturates substance, brings it to life, and then causes it to grow and develop in an organic way."

Chapter 12. Mystical Practices

Mystical practices refer to the attainment of insight in ultimate or hidden truths and is the key to human transformation. It is supported by various experiences and disciplined practices that unfold and cultivate the power of the mystical senses. It is through Ho'omana Kahiko with which the miracles of healing, prophecy, interaction and illumination are achieved. For this reason, it is a lifelong process of learning and deep contemplation, which must not be taken lightly or played as an ego-driven competitive game.

Establishing direct Power Contact with Hika-Po-Loa (the Divine Trinity) provides for unfoldment of mystical abilities. The I'O, or resident God Light within the human body, is the spiritual monitor of its senses. It is expressed through sight, hearing, touch, taste, smell, and your sense of time and space.

Expansion of consciousness awareness is the enhancement of any and all senses. When used in the service of counseling and healing, they can be developed as extraordinary powers, and in some religions are considered to be *Gifts of the Spirit*, which create an effect or an extraordinary event. Unfolding your abilities through mystical practices is a lifelong journey of cultivating your natural resources from within. Each of your normal physical senses has its deeper metaphysical counterpart, which expand with intent to serve humanity. The following describe mystical abilities and identify related principles, which unfold shamanic healing skills through mystical practices.

Mystical Practices Chart

Mana Ability	Principle: Psychic Healing Skills
1. **Seeing**	**Ike:** Clairvoyance. Sees clearly in any reality and from many perspectives, perceive Divine purpose, an adventurer, sees beyond with all senses
2. **Clearing**	**Kala:** Shifts dis-ease conditions, cleanses, releases mental/physical blocks, clears all PEMS channels, transmits, transforms
3. **Focusing**	**Makia:** Holds attention, focused intent, manifest events, changes weather, heals, brings prosperity, transforms, shapeshifts
4. **Presence**	**Manawa:** Beingness, be present in the Presence, Divine connection in the now, the moment of power, uplifts all things, higher consciousness
5. **Blessing**	**Aloha:** Peacemaker, love, joy, inspiration, transmits curative mana, reinforces actual and potential good, invokes Divine Presence
6. **Empower**	**Mana:** Generates and emanates inner power to external manifestation, empowers all people, places, and things
7. **Effective**	**Pono:** Weaves existing consciousness, teaches, integrates first 6 abilities, uses imagination with the goal of pono
8. **Manifest**	**Ho'omana:** Actualizes higher consciousness (IAO) to create mana in all realities (physical, psychic, symbolic, oneness and dream), manifest, adapt, convert disempowerment to empowerment

"Think about it, and it will think about you. Live it and it will live for you. Apply it in any direction, and it will apply itself in that direction for you. Praise it and it will praise you. There is nothing that it will not do for you, in as much as you would do for yourself."

- Kahu Abraham Kawaii

Discipline: Inner Work – Ulukau and Ike Papalua

Ulukau means having intuitive abilities and the definition of *Ike Papalua* is having second sight (psychic ability). Cultivating ulukau and ike papalua increases your capability to connect to the place where truth lives. Psyche means soul. Psychic ability is manifestation of the soul. An intuitive or psychic can enter the stream of thought of anyone whose vibration he or she can mentally contact, whether that person is in the flesh or out of it. Since everyone is psychic, we are all communicating with each other constantly. This means every human being has inherent psychic powers and all use them in one-way or another. In some, these innate faculties are developed knowingly and with acceptance from birth. Others may have to work hard and require a longer period of patient cultivation to trust them. This provides opportunity to expand consciousness awareness tools through the disciplines of inner work practices.

Many people love the game of tennis. Those who want to play well professionally read the instructions; take lessons from the best, and practice daily. It is the same for unfolding mystical abilities for spiritual work. Study to become knowledgeable. Investigate your natural abilities and learn how best to unfold them to achieve your goals. If you do not have a goal to serve others, you may miss the very purpose of being a shaman candidate and can easily develop a lower psychicism, whereby the ego is the driving force. Know your Self. Be mindful about how you innately function. Honor your sensitivities and discover more about you and how you are called to serve.

While you are yet *Holona Noi'i*, a Novice Scholar, unskilled in the esoteric power, it is important that you discover how to support your spiritual and material vision and mission through *ho'o lokahi*. Ho'o lokahi is the causal action of oneness with the higher dimensions that generates agreement, diversity, and unity. It is this essence of unity, which embraces and honors diversity of thought before expansion of consciousness can occur. Develop mystical attributes by unfolding them through daily *pa hana ko'iko'i* (inner work discipline). Do the work; the rest will follow. The following disciplines are preparation for mystical service.

Discipline: The Eye of Kanaloa

Courtesy of Serge King **The Eye is Insight and More...**

The higher consciousness grid of the Eye of Kanaloa represents the aka web, or the web of life; the symbolic connection of all things to each other. It is your personal energetic life grid integrating Spirit. A shaman star at the center depicts the spider/shaman, or the person who is aware of his or her own life as a Dreamweaver.

According to a Kauai tradition, if you could look into the eye of Kanaloa you would see this pattern. The star is composed of a dot representing the Aumakua, or Higher Self in the center. It is our *Nana I Ke Kumu* – Nana, meaning to see or look to the source. This is the nucleus, the core, the heart, the focus. A ring symbolizes Lono, or the Mental Self; the seven limbs of the star correspond to the first seven principles; and the ring around the star represents Ku, the Physical or Subconscious Self. One point of the star is always pointed down, aligned with a straight line of the web, representing the connection of the inner with the outer and the eight lines represent mana, or spiritual power. Another meaning of mana is conveyed in the branching lines and the number eight in Hawaiian tradition is a symbol of great power. The four circles represent the practice of aloha, or love since the lei or garland is a circular symbol of love. *Ha* is an empowering part of the word aloha, which means breath, life and the number four. The circles and lines represent the harmony of love and power as an ideal oneness to develop.

The Kanaloa symbol generates subtle energy, which can be used for healing, for stimulating physical and mental faculties, and for many other purposes. The symbolic connection to all things harmonizes the physical, emotional and mental energies of any location. The ancient grid is also the background for the official seal and emblem of the United Nations. Two olive branches encircle the web of higher consciousness signifying peace and unity conveying the hopes and dreams. The global map signifies all people and countries.

Connecting with the Shaman Star

The shaman star (*hoku malama*) represents the Higher Self. Mystically it means an illuminated body, or causing enlightenment. The 7-pointed star speaks to your ability to function from the power of the Shaman Within. The very center of the eye is the star gate of the Eye of Kanaloa, which integrates the Divine with the Material.

The shaman star symbol is depicted in the awesome connection within the universe. The center is Universal Mind, God/IAO. The Divine radiates through all that is. The circles or rings within the star draw you into the heart of the universe. This is where you can access the inner circles of consciousness, which pulsates throughout all. The spirals stimulate transformation, healing and change and are activated through the process of sensing truth. You can perceive yourself through the mystical point in meditation as you concentrate on the center point within the inner circles to use as an internally directed metaphysical tool. When you think you are there, relax and go deeper. When you experience the shaman star as your *Star-Self*, you are a mirror of the cosmos incarnated. The deeper you go into your inner consciousness, the more it brings you into the realm of Being and the need to anchor it into the material world through service.

Before you begin to learn what you think are shaman skills in methods, rituals or techniques, it is imperative that you pull yourself into that mystical star within yourself. This is where you open to the Light of your own soul and unfold your extra-ordinary Shaman Self through the infinite Aka link establishing direct power contact with Hika-Po-Loa. Discover your physical, metaphysical, symbolic, oneness and dream expertise through understanding the five levels of reality. Explore the ideal state of your three selves to function as one cohesive unit. Be mindful to always be in touch with who you are at your core, and be connected to why you incarnated. It is up to you to perceive your own destiny. If you don't know that, this is your first assignment.

Tapping into the hidden factor in your mystical abilities unfoldment starts when your desire is for *kokua* service (extending loving help to others). Think about ways you can function most effectively. You might ask the question, "What do people really need from me?" Then, discover how you can prepare to serve their needs. It is through disciplined effort, that your capability to serve others will be formed. It is an ongoing, ever unfolding process that your will perpetuates once you have found answers from within.

The most effective shaman tools are developed through the assistance of the Higher Self and are expressed in many subtle ways. Lokahi is the medium with which to bridge from the chaos of density into the unity of higher consciousness. As you become familiar with this meditative approach, you may simply imagine through your mind's eye or follow the traditions of old to use the actual stars in the heavens as your focus. The shaman star also directs your attention to empowering principles of enlightenment. Once you have reached direct power contact, use the 8th principle to create reality from Divine Source. There are four interconnected areas in the disciplines needing your attention that must be balanced and harmonized. These are: Ka Kino, the body; Ka Mana'o, the mind; Ka Uhane, the spirit; and Ka Honua, the world. Expand them in Kahuna consciousness.

Discipline: Meditation - No'ono'o Pono

> "It is through meditation that we are spiritually guided. Meditation is the time when you are directly in touch with the aumakua, directly in touch with the gods. ...To fully charge, or recharge your psychic and spiritual batteries, you must plan to invest a full 30 minutes per day, an hour if possible, in sincere prayer communication with Aumakua, with Hika-Po-Loa, and with those other divine contacts indicated or dictated by your Priestly or Lay vocation and/or avocation."
>
> - Lanakila Brandt

No'ono'o means thought, reflection, thinking and meditation. Another way to say this is *No'ono'o pono*, to think carefully, meditate, and concentrate. A process of meditation creates a doorway to go within. It is an essential discipline to find inner peace and of taking steps to power on the narrow path of the Kahuna. Meditation is the sacred path of becoming aligned with your Self, harmony with others, in balance with your environment, and attuned with your God. The novice prepares by opening to sensing truth from within as it is revealed in the meditative tools of Breath, Light, Sound and Pule (prayer).

Discipline: Walking Meditation – Hele Noonoo Ana

Hele noonoo ana means walking meditation. Taking a daily walk with Spirit establishes a consistent connection with the higher realm. It is a scheduled appointment between you and your higher helpers. The walk in nature perpetuates a valuable meditative life. Plan for a walking meditation period in which to tap into your own richness, depth, and understanding. Shift into a higher state of awareness while walking with Spirit. This and other daily rituals will help you attune to the voices of the Divine in a conversing method for contemplation or avenue for interactive meditations. It is a way to tend to your Light:

> The first half of the walk is dedicated to talking. Talk to God, your Aumakua, inner selves, guides, totems, angels, ancestors or the Universe in general. Talk about what is going on in your life, or what you want or think you need. Talk about anything that is important to you or anything that comes into your mind.
>
> The second half of the walk is for listening. Observe everything your guides or the Universe expresses to you. Experience your feelings, attune to sensations in your body, hear sounds around you, smell aromas, and take in the sights. Become an instrument of listening, observing and absorbing everything in your awareness.

Discipline: Expanded Awareness – Hakalau

In Hawaiian spirituality, Hakalau means expanded awareness or to enter a deeper state of consciousness at will. It is also referred to as *Kahuna Consciousness* since it is through expanded consciousness that the Kahuna is able to manifest mana and perform the magical elements of mind/body/spirit physical healing and empowerment processes. Kahuna Consciousness is a defined concept, which addresses human awareness of both internal and external stimuli and behaviors. This relates to spiritual recognition, altered states, psychological understanding, and in our modern concepts today, relates to our life purpose, satisfaction, and self-actualization.

The mystical Kupua is on a dedicated journey of expanded consciousness. When you follow it, your capacity to receive mana expands with the increase of spiritual awareness and your ability to intake Divine energy, which enlightens your consciousness. Your conscious awakening encompasses all the abilities to express spiritual enlightenment to assist others. Spiritual development increases your ability to express mana used in healing and all transformations. It is one of the most effective tools in the modern and ancient practice of the empowerments because it entails actually functioning on a different level of awareness. Operating in a higher conscious awareness directly contributes to the success of anything and everything you do in shaman service. It harmonizes and balances by lifting everyone and everything into a higher state of aloha/loving, lokahi/unity and pono/loving action. Use kaona (deepening) in these areas:

- Communicate with your High Self
- Get to know the inner you
- Use as a development tool for yourself
- Learn to connect to the deeper part within
- Conduct ho'ola (healing) sessions

The deeper level of Hakalua training from Uncle George Naope teaches that when in the kaona (deeper) state of Hakalau, you open your mind to possibilities beyond the normal range of your usual limited mind-brain function. Trance and shamanic states of consciousness are part of the forgotten human genetic structure by which you function in a higher state of awareness.

With practice, you can enter into this expanded awareness at will. Study the practices of ancient temple LomiLomi, Kahi Loa, and Ha'a Hula to use kaona methods that train you to access and function in Kahuna consciousness. This normal state of higher consciousness alertness can be a viable part of your spiritual practice expertise. Always remember that trance is a *normal function* of life, which many go into automatically upon relaxing. As a practitioner, it is important for you to learn what trance is and know when you or your client moves or shifts into any different range of brain activity. Seek instruction from a Hawaiian teacher or qualified hypnosis instructor to learn to work with the deepest part of your higher mind. Dr. Paul Milton Carter, Ph.D., *Trance and Healing Instruction* says:

> "Trance is one of the best tools you can learn, both for self-help and as a body worker, therapist or healer. It improves the effectiveness of any form of therapy by helping you to utilize the creative and integrative powers of the unconscious, and freeing and fortifying the natural immune system."

Discipline: HA Breath - Higher Consciousness Access

The sacred breath or Spirit is Alo, called HA Breath, the Divine breath of life (higher consciousness). When Alo is present, the most sacred thing you can do is breathe. HA Breath provides access to the higher consciousness that is within each of us. When you are functioning from your Divine Self, each time you inhale and exhale HA Breath is conveyed. The point is to be knowingly connected to the Divine as you breathe. This basic concept in the HA Breathing practice is the dominant Hawaiian belief that God is inside us. To access your divinity, you need to breathe, which in turn permeates you and everything in your environment. The result is that you consciously know and act from the level of the Spirit within yourself. A simple practice of connecting to Source is to breathe in a complete cycle. Breathe in through the nose and out through the mouth thirty times. As you consciously breathe outward, make a *hah* sound (as yawning) coming from deep inside yourself. When you feel fully charged, relax your structured breathing. Breathe in your normal rhythm, keeping your thoughts focused on Divine purpose as you prepare to do your sacred work.

Discipline: Connect, Ground, and Function From Source

Your breath and process of breathing creates mana for all activities. It only takes a moment to purposefully connect to and be able to function through your higher consciousness self. Realize when you do, you actually function *as* Divine Spirit. When you are cut off from the flow of life force, you will notice your breathing becomes shallow and in fact, you will at times hold your breath. Ha Breathing generates the source of mana (life force) causing these effects:

- Ha Breath (higher consciousness) with intent creates
- Haole Breath (lower consciousness) is the root of suffering
- When the mind thinks, the body automatically inhales
- When the body exhales, it automatically sends a message to transform thought into material form
- Be mindful of what you think and breathe out into the universe, for it affects all life, including your own

Discipline: HA Mo'o Breath Technique

The *ha mo'o* form of meditation is one in which the essence of life and the evolutionary process unfold in alternate states of being. It shifts consciousness. Before undertaking a task or to support the mana needs of others, the ancients gathered to breathe together for hours to generate *alo*/higher consciousness mana. To connect with your Higher Self, take four HA Breaths. Breathe in deeply with focused intent. Extend the exhale breath two or more counts longer than the inhalation. Relax with each deep breath and hold the intention to connect with your Higher Self. Notice that your state of consciousness immediately shifts to engage with the intention you have chosen. The dynamics of HA Breath cultivate a higher consciousness mana in the breaths, and connects intent with I'O, the core of your High Self. The result:

- HA Breath is an automatic connection with your Higher Self, to be in Oneness, and to function in Kahuna consciousness, which transforms
- HA Breath creates a connection in the PEMS (physical, emotional, mental, and spiritual) channels
- HA Breath rekindles an ancient health practice that calms the mind and soothes the soul

One method uses the words Alo**ha** and Ma**ha**lo or Lo**ka**hi as an intention to engage higher consciousness in HA Breath:

- *Alo**ha*** transforms the unloving into lovingness
- Lo**ka**hi transmits the principle of **ka** (essence of mana) oneness in the breath of life
- Ma**ha**lo expresses gratitude. "Thank you," is a blessing for the future: "May the breath of life stay with you"

Discipline: Light Alignment – Ho'opololei

Ho'opololei means to straighten. The Light restores and aligns the sacred Bowl of Light. It permeates everything. It is always accessible. It is within every human to allow the Light to glow brightly. Two practices in aligning light are La'akea and Malama, the radiating of Light.

La'akea – Divine Light: La'akea means God Light. La means God. Akea is Light. La'akea is the actual energy of Divine Source (Holy Spirit). This powerful aligning meditation restores harmony and balance to quickly bring ho'oponopono within. See yourself surrounded with Divine Light. Allow the Light to spread around you and radiate inside you. It will cleanse, harmonize, and fill you with Love.

Malama – Radiating of Light: The discipline of Light includes aligning of malamalama. Malamalama is the Light of knowledge, clarity of thinking, enlightenment and radiance. Malamalama energy assists you in living your intention to serve others. It is the Light of the sun radiating outward to manifest in the physical world and the moon illuminating the inner awareness. Establish contact with your Aumakua for Spirit blessings to flow as malamalama permeates all.

Discipline: Sacred Sounds

> "He who knows the secret of sound knows the Mystery of the whole universe."
> - Hazrat Inavat Khan

Form and sound are essential keys for the aspiring Hawaiian Rite practitioner. In the ancient world, Sound is the Word. The flow of mana (life force) generates, transmits and transmutes naturally through sound and vibration. In ordinary daily life, sound is a natural flowing energy emanating from everything. There are tones that carry meanings within meanings and also those that transmit vibrational consciousness of mana that heal and also emit frequencies that destroy. The native people believed that sound was spirit made manifest. Sound is effective in direct proportion to the mana flow in the person when pule (prayer) and ceremonies are performed from a place of sacredness. You have the ability to generate and control the consciousness level of the sound within you and the reverberation that you create. Whether the specific sound uttered is purposeful or created unknowingly, consciousness moves accordingly. The shaman changes mana flow consciously in the manner he or she speaks or forms the vowels, frames specific consonants, and positions words together.

Discipline: Sacred Sounds in Vowels

Vowels carry meaning and form. The most sacred of sounds in the Hawaiian language are I, A, and O (ancient name of God). Explore the meaning held within these vowels:

I Sound: Ee as in we – Response: When you call out in fright, "Eek! It's a mouse!" I (Ee) means in, on, at or to. The esoteric meaning aligns the possible with spirit fulfillment, passion, creativity, and expression. The action is to open up, awaken the inner fire, turn up the pilot light, and give energy. It summons the creative forces, ignites and fans it, enticing the flames of the Aumakua within.

E Sound: Ay as in way – Response: "Let's smooth things out." Sacred meaning is an announcement, calling attention to the Divine and spreading out mana resulting in peace, serenity, calmness and ease. This calls sacred consciousness to express inner stillness qualities of the Divine Aumakua within.

A Sound: Ah as jaw, law - Response: When you understand something, you say, "Ah" or "Aha!" Sacred meanings: awakening to the Divine, the esoteric meaning of God, divinity, sunlight, enlighten, awaken, receptivity, nurture and understand.

O Sound: Oh as in whole. Sacred meanings: The Divine, wholeness, well rounded, complete and the Source. Use in emanating the Divine Aumakua wholeness within.

U Sound: Oo as in new, renew. Sacred meanings: activating mana, radiation from source, empowerment and realization resulting in transformation, vitality, inspiration and magnificence. Use to generate Divine Energy for a multitude of purposes including causing growth, magic, shapeshifting and dimensional travel, which are actual skills of the spiritually evolved human.

Discipline: Chanting (Oli)

The significance of the Hawaiian Oli (chant) was felt in every aspect of Hawaiian culture and tradition. Life and spirituality were communicated through poetic stories covering genealogies, powerful chiefs, accounts of beauty of various lands, and to express love. The Oli contains layers of hidden meanings that often wove kaona (double meanings), creating multiple translations. This modern IAO Chant uses the innermost sacred sounds to bring forth meaning and mana to heal. God (IAO) is spread through the mind, body, and spirit, and permeates all.

IAO Chant: EEEEEAAAAHOOOH (Chant seven times)

Sound	Focus
EEE	Crown
AAA	Third eye
AAH	Heart
OO	Solar plexus
OH	Mana exchange with Source

Discipline: Pule – Effective Prayer Action

> "Prayer is access to all that you are - and all that you are not aware of being."
> — Kahu Abraham Kawaii

In all effective prayer action, it is essential to reach in sincerity further than your limited consciousness to link to Infinite Source, which goes beyond your mind to the Great Power of the Universe. The effective prayer connects to the High Self. The meaning of the word prayer is an earnest request. *Waipa* and *Pule* are two significant Hawaiian references for prayer:

- Waipa is a request, a prayer. Waipa literally means to divide water. Water is the Hawaiian symbol for mana or vital force. This type of prayer connection taps into and activates mana.

- A Pule brings the prayer intent into center-point, which is a focused intent that manifests a cohesive hearts desire with mana. It means to send forth. Pule means to cast a magic spell, incantation, incantation, blessing, grace, and church service, as well as, to pray, worship, say grace, or ask a blessing.

A pule or prayer is a direct connection with Spirit (akua, gods, angel, guides, and ancestors). The most powerful prayer action happens spontaneously in your thoughts every moment of the day. Spontaneous means when pule is done without a lot of planning. To be effective, thoughts and prayers must be in alignment with your hopes and dreams during each moment. Your thinking is creating prayer at all times, as well as when you orchestrate a formal pule. Giving blessings is an effective, immediate prayer. Keep in mind that every thought, whether positive (blessing) or negative (curse) is a command that will strengthen or transform something.

Formalized prayer refers to a carefully orchestrated ritual, which is a blueprint for the design of what is to be built. It is spoken or chanted statements and affirms intention to the High Self. All external prayer ritual is simply for the dramatic effect it has on the human process itself. Steps of effective prayer action include deciding a plan for your future. This is another way of saying that you must be aware of who you are and why you came to this planet and create your prayers in accordance with what you want to achieve in fulfilling the purpose for your life.

Purposefully use visual and verbal diagrams to build a set of thought-forms, which include details to bring the desired condition into the reality of your belief system. Visualize your prayers as seeds growing to become the present. Use physical stimuli to impress your subconscious with determination and passion. Prioritize your requests; state what is desired and the intended result. Never ask for anything to knowingly hurt another. Remove any blocks that may prevent manifestation. Blocks are caused by fixed ideas held in density. They appear as fixations, fear, guilt, and addiction that demand specific results. Kala (forgiveness) is an integral part of prayer. The formula given by Kumukahi Educators *Olelo No'eau #1230 is:*

> ***I luna na maka, I lalo na kuli***
> Eyes up, knees down. Pray.

Discipline: Haipule – Activating Prayer

Ha i pule means to say prayer employing the power of higher consciousness. The Ha prefix adds the mana of "*Ha*" and meaning of "*I*" (possible, potential). To say prayers the shaman way is more extensive than just using words; it means really give full voice and use Mind/Body/Spirit to activate prayer in multiple ways. The Kupua connects with all the senses, generating and directing mana from all dimensions. The process invokes a psychological procedure that employs the intent of our minds that manifest transformation and healing through the strength of the right, desire, will, and power.

The Haipule Process

Root	Significance	Instruction
Ha:	Life, breath, spirit	Breathe deeply. Get excited
I:	Speak the possible	Describe what you want
Pu:	Issue forth, emanate	Imagine what you want
Le:	To move, cause	Take action confidently

Declare Prayer (Bless) – Activate All Levels

Activate	Ignite and stimulate what you want
Verbalize	Express what you want
Symbolize	Signify meaning of what you want
Visualize	Diagram what you want
Actualize	Actuate dream: Create what you want

Divination - Kilokilo

Shamanism is a system of knowledge and divination is one of the ways to gain direct knowledge. Divination is simply a way of revealing the truth. The diviner accesses hidden truths or the circumstances surrounding them. Hawaiians used many forms of divination (*kilokilo*) to divine truth. Their intuitive sense was keenly sharpened by everyday life where everything that exists is alive. They read astrology directly from the stars, planets, and the moon. *Polynesian Religion* tells that in every form of activity, work, war, play, and love, there were innumerable special omens. Every person, and particularly every leader, was their own diviner of truth and capable of being their own prophet.

Kupua Stones - Toss-The-Rocks

By Rev. Rebecca Thompson
Founder of TAGA

Through the invocation of Spirit and Divine Magic Shaman Stones Divination is a life transforming healing technique that creates a new life blueprint aligned to one's heart desire. Within Sacred Space and with Divine Assistance an Energetic Life Grid is created and Shaman Stones are identified as life aspects, players, and components. Then the Shaman Stones are tossed onto the grid thus presenting "what is" in one's field of play. Once all is revealed, the Magical Alchemy begins with optimizing and declaring "what will be." Then with the invocation of the Divine, the new life blueprint is anchored into the "here and now."

Kupua means to bring forth; to teach. It is a divination tool that has been handed down for centuries in many different cultures and traditions to tell the story of alignment: What is now and what is intended to be. I fondly call this method "Toss-The-Rocks," which is the use of tossing several multi-colored Shaman Stones to reveal energetic, relational consciousness within each person's grid of light.

Toss-The-Rocks Process

Before tossing the rocks, it is recommended that each participant becomes as "present" as possible by connecting (grounding) fully to Mother Earth, and then gently running energy up the energetic spine to each of the chakras, and finally reaching the higher chakras by connecting to Father Sky. Once this connection happens, bring the energy back down, pooling for a moment at the 3rd eye, and finally resting at the heart chakra. The process:

1. **Intention Is Everything**! The person is encouraged to bring their awareness (their consciousness) to the question at hand. This intention focuses their light lines that hold both the known and unknown consciousness held in their grid of light.
    a. The person in the "role of the Shaman" also intends to connect to the person's grid of light, as well as, intends to connect to the Divine.

- ❖ Think of connecting to avatars, guides, angels, and shamans that are there to assist, so the answers come from the Divine into the receiver's 3rd eye and heart chakra and not into the "logical" mind.
2. The Shaman energizes the stones to be used on behalf of the other person, by intending the stones to reveal their "points of light consciousness" and hands the stones over to the person who has the question.
3. The Shaman directs the person to hold the stones and the stones begin to resonate to the person's light grid.
    a. The person is generally not aware of it, but what they are doing when they hold the stones, is that they are aligning their conscious vibration with their question and each of the components within their question links to each of the stones.
    b. This conscious vibration becomes separate "points of light" within their grid. Think of it as "packets" of consciousness that vibrate to the essence of each assigned meaning, such as an obstacle, a friend, having access to abundance consciousness, or right source of income and so forth.
4. The Shaman directs the person to bring their awareness (consciousness) to their questions by having the person assign a meaning to each stone, such as obstacle, family, friends, and/or outcomes.
    a. For each question, the Shaman encourages the person to assign as many possible components there are within the question, which will help reveal more of a robust and comprehensive pattern of relational consciousness.
    b. If there are several components, it's a good idea to write down what each stone/color represents because it sometimes gets very hard to remember "what is what" when your 3rd eye is being flooded with information and the logical mind is trying to put patterns into place that may or may not be accurate.
    c. It's also a good idea to write out what the question is, because many times, you will find a revealing of not what their out-loud question is, but what the

unspoken heart question is, which of course is *the Real Question* they really wanted to know.

5. The Shaman directs the person to cup all the assigned stones and to gently shake them all up. If they're confused, have them think of shaking up dice. The Shaman encourages the person to say out loud "Stones please reveal the light points of my question" and then state their question out loud.
6. The person then gently tosses the stones onto a flat surface; a pattern of relational consciousness will emerge.
7. The Reveal: Interpretation and Divination:
    a. The closer the stones are to each other, the closer the connection, attraction or alignment it is showing; conversely, the farther away, indicates a weaker connection or less of a charge in consciousness.
       ❖ Think of magnets (attractions or aversions).
    b. If the stones are showing "right side up," the consciousness is in the "here and now."
    c. If the stones drop "upside down," the consciousness is in the "place of possibilities," another way of saying it, "it's in the Spirit World" or "Divine."
       ❖ Think "as above, so below." People often forget how much they create in the Spirit world which creates everything in the here and now.
    d. Look for geometric patterns: circles, triangles, and squares, straight lines, which show additional layers within a relationship. For example:
       ❖ Three points creating a triangle and a third point is way off in the distance shows how the three points of light have a closer relationship than the one off in the distance. Many times, the top of the triangle is in the Spirit World, where the other two points are in the here and now.
    e. It's amazing how many hidden questions are answered, just by observing the patterns and the relationship each stone (each packet of consciousness) has to one another.
8. The Shaman's role is to really encourage the person to connect to and review what their light pattern is showing

them. It is to also help them seek and express their own interpretation and their own course of action because:
   a. The more intentionally the person can connect to their grid, the deeper the consciousness will shift when relational light points are moved within the grid.
   b. It also helps to encourage the person to open up and fully connect to the "field of play" as all packets of their consciousness can be modified through their own intention.

A sense of wonder and playfulness is important to this process! The client is asked to get into the essence of the issue in their heart. The client picks up their stones and throws them like dice. The pattern and relationships between the stones are interpreted: the closeness of people, whether the stones are in the physical world or spiritual, the location of obstacles relative to people and concepts... Upon tossing them, the consciousness of the stones have a life and animation of their own.

The shift in the clients can come by playing with the position and relationship and even removing stones from that stage. You can flip the physical/spiritual state. You can adjust relationships by changing the proximity of stones. You can block or unblock relations. Within this grid of light, if you know a healing modality such as Huna, Reiki, Yuen method, Matrix Energetics, or provide energetic healing etc., you can do energetic modifications to delete negative emotions, clear and strengthen the thing that any stone represents as well as the change of relationships between stones. Strengthening can be achieved by moving concepts like unconditional love closer, even touching a person's stone.

In the Shamanic role, the Shaman knows that all healing modalities lead first with bridging one's consciousness to the Divine, the place of intention; to help bring forth into the "here and now" new energetic shifts in consciousness, to balance and strengthen for a more aligned outcome on behalf of the person. The Shaman can either help the person do it themselves or provide Hawaiian healing modalities: Haipule, prayer, or Kino Mana (body work) of LomiLomi or Kahi Loa (healing with the elements). The Shaman knows that all shifts in consciousness (all healings) come from Divine Grace and the Shaman is nothing more than a bridge into this amazing and the wonderful state of Grace. Blessed Be!

Discipline: Hula – Spiritual Practice

The hula dance is one of Hawaii's oldest cultural traditions and spiritual practices characterized by rhythmic body movement and hand gestures. It is the expression of our thoughts, feelings, and experiences. The poetic chant or mele accompanies the hula and drumming is used to increase energy and sustain focus into the purpose for the dance. The public performance of hula has four purposes: to entertain, inspire, instruct, and for worship. According to the intention of the practitioner, hula expresses pleasant feelings and power that shifts consciousness for healing, whether it is in telling a story, giving joyful performance, or in worshipful devotion. The ancient transformative and healing practice is not just a dance; it is the movement of consciousness. The root meaning is:

Hu - spreading outward – movement
La - God

Hula means *God in us* and is the actuality of God energy flowing in and through the body. Hula is felt as God-movement through its spiritual purpose: the spreading out of the light to cause enlightenment. The Hawaiian dance is also an expression of rotational magnetic energy that transmits. It generates healing according to the consciousness of the dancer. All dancers are practitioners of consciousness on some level; many are unaware they convey mana as do Kahuna Kupua.

Hula in Reality Levels

There are many levels of hula and it's healing practices today as in ancient times. Because hula is a mana flowing system of esoteric dimension, it is effective in multiple levels of reality, which touches all people at one level or another. This is how I see the effects of hula in reality levels:

1. Physical Reality Mana flow tones muscles, increases flexibility and oxygenates the entire body through the deep breathing, stamina and mind-set needed to dance.
2. Psychic Reality Mana flow opens the material as well as spiritual worlds to connect with everyone and everything in metaphysical communication.
3. Symbolic Reality conveys meaning in every movement, gives messages and also tells a story quite clearly.
4. Oneness Mana flow-generating practice merges everyone into the sense of unity as in a powerful hypnotic trance.
5. Dream Reality Mana flow shifts consciousness in all expressions to create and integrate in all frameworks.

Modern Shaman Practice of Hula Movement

The traditional Hawaiian dance is a system of shamanism and a dramatic ritualistic way of emanating mana, dependent on the dancer's ability to focus his or her consciousness in the moment. You can practice the mana movement wherever you go and whatever you do. It provides:

- A ritualistic way of opening to the Divine
- A way to attune to the Divine
- An empowering stream of consciousness
- Radiating to share with others
- Weaving mana into each moment
- Energy to flow in each movement
- Manifesting intention through focused consciousness

Hula - An Energy Generating Practice

Hula is an energy generating practice. The energetics of dancing hula is a complete body, mind and spirit workout. It stimulates virtually every system within the body by increasing oxygen and blood flow, loosening joints, strengthening bones and muscles, focusing the mind, and increasing the depths of one's spiritual experience. Hula for your spiritual development and for healing is very simple and very powerful through the shifting of mana. It can be practiced anytime by anyone. This process transcends religious beliefs. However, if you choose to do so, you can incorporate your religious values, prayers, attunements and even channel the energy of God, angels, guides and ancestors into your practice. Everyone, on some level or another, radiates mana and moves consciousness through their body. Consciousness radiates outwardly even when you sit in stillness and circulates more when you consciously move with intention. It reasons that when you are connected to Divine Source, even moving a finger constitutes healing through the shifting of mana flowing and also directs consciousness through your mind and body. Whenever you purposefully embody the vital life force and direct Divine energy through thought or the very action of movement, it becomes a powerful transmission of energy. This conveys the vital force to the purpose intended.

Discipline: Ha'a – Sacred Movement

Ha'a Movement is so ancient that it is very little known outside Hawaii today. It is a deeply sacred worship practice performed in the temple Ha'a form, under the direction of a Kahuna priest or public mele practice. I actually danced Ha'a in trance before I knew anything about Hawaiian shamanism. Ha'a is still a means to channel Divine energy today, which actually shifts and changes consciousness as it permeates and transforms density within yourself and others to vitalize and heal. In the practice of ancient Ha'a, the following transformations have been observed:

> "Plants, which usually do not bloom, do bloom. Flowers on plants that normally do not have an aroma, spontaneously begin to emit a fragrance."

Ha'a movement brings the ancient worship into a public format that demonstrates all of life is spiritual. It is no longer hidden in private temple ritual. Now all the world is the temple. Dancing in a spontaneous free-form channeling of energy is practiced all over the world. Friends of ours get together in Camp Verde, Arizona, during open mic sessions. The musicians play and sing and when the audience can't sit still any longer, they just get up and dance. When my husband, Ron McLain, performs, he often finds me dancing hula to his rendition of *Georgia*, dancing as the Spirit moves. To my great joy a lovely lady named Leah also danced. She moved in a mesmerizing way, directing energy with her hands. It was graceful and powerful.

One day Leah shared with me that the movement she was doing came from her African heritage, a process of clearing, balancing, and healing, which was quite similar to Ha'a movement. We often danced at the same time, showering each other with African and Hawaiian gestures. People loved to see her dance. Her husband, Lance, wrote a song called *When Leah Dances*. The energy in the room still changes when she dances and everyone feels better. What most people don't know is that Leah is a modern shaman. She doesn't have to tell people. They just know something magical happens when Leah dances. As Leah shows, Ha'a is utilized by other cultures.

Anyone can move the life force through their body with serious intention. You can start with Haipule to be filled with mana. However, when you simply stand, you automatically circulate mana flow that you have generated. Hula allows gravity to move through the hips and the movement of the mana continues flowing through shifting weight to the right side and left side of your body. This also draws life force from the earth; it flows up through the body, through the arms and in doing so, directs it where you want it to go. As you do, you gather more mana in the process. Accordingly, consciously living hula is one of the deeply moving and transformative mystical skills. Hula becomes a natural process in your life that can be a conduit of higher energy (literally, higher consciousness) in yourself and for others. Modern shamanism integrates the practice of hula (moving of mana) with other practices. The movement also gracefully spreads harmony and balance through the medium of a most pleasant and loving activity as you integrate it into every moment of your life.

Discipline: Temple Healing Practices

All temple healing practices are forms of prayer. Hawaiian Temple healing is a profound transformative spiritual practice of movement of consciousness, which activates on a cellular and molecular level as well as through the emotional, mental, spiritual, and physical bodies. It is recommended that the student receive Hawaiian temple healing procedures as effective restorative and life changing sessions and as a part of their personal development; then include the instruction in their shamanic preparation curriculum. Hawaiian Temple healing is enhanced through attuning to the Elements and the five major levels of reality. It is extremely effective in teaching and preparing the practitioner to enter into the appropriate state of consciousness for being in service.

Temple Kahi Loa

Kahi Loa is a shamanic form of Hawaiian sacred practices that bring transformation and healing. As the recipient selects an intention or goal for the session, the practitioner employs the Mana (Divine Power) of Spirit in the expressions of Fire, Wind, Water, Earth, Plants, Animals and People to harmonize and balance. Kahi Loa is a deep, gentle, loving communion with Nature and one's soul using light touches on the skin of the fully clothed recipient. Kahi Loa came from the healing traditions of the Kahili family through Serge Kahili King. Susan Pa'iniu Floyd added the spiritual dimensions of temple style, which activate the actual channeling of the elements of Nature. The Elements work within the scope of both practitioner and receiver through the interconnectedness and dedication of loving service. Refer to the Elements of Nature Chart in the Kalana Hula Meditation to invite attunement with each.

Temple Lomi

A Kahuna Lomi Lomi specializes in bodywork to restore balance in order that mana (life energy) can flow effectively. Described by Kumu Floyd of Aloha International, as *Lomi Nui*, it is a graceful, in-depth bodywork called Kino Mana. This modality incorporates ha'a (temple hula) practice to produce a profound regenerative effect for the recipient while also energizing the practitioner. It is a massage-like spiritual practice whereby the practitioner is the dancer who generates a higher consciousness field as the subconscious of the recipient orchestrates the session. The practitioner employs the Kupua principles of attentiveness, love and respect. The Kahuna Kupua Shaman practiced a unique modality called *Ke Ala Hoku, Pathway to the Stars*, a form of Temple bodywork that carries you to your true nature. The healing arts from all lineages and traditions are the fundamental tools for serving the Spirit of Aloha. The temple healing tradition presents the receiver an empowerment of being a temple, and taking on the responsibility of committing to the spiritual practice of loving one's self as an instrument of enlightenment. Kupua Wayne Powell says:

> "In practice, it has little to do with massage, and everything to do with embarking on a journey that regenerates your wholeness from within. Assisted by guardian spirits, we uncover your innate innocence that arises from the memory and experience of being one with God."

Discipline: Revelatory Dream – Moe'uhane

Many indigenous people believed as some ancient Hawaiians, that life starts when you go to sleep at night. During sleep, you live your life and in the morning, you use that energy to carry out your life in physical form during the day. Other beliefs were that life is actually a dream that we create. So, the people looked at what they saw as their experience of reality; their outer world, as a reflection of their inner world, confirmed by their beliefs, thoughts, and ideas about life. If they wanted to change something on the outside, they would start by looking inside to change their belief, thought or idea. The basic thread is that we create our own reality at night and during the daytime dream. In the Foreword to the book *Hawaiian Legends of Dreams* by Caren Loebel-Fried, Keola Beamer said:

> "Dreams are the beginning. They are the seed of our ambitions, the source of our inspiration, and the impetus for our creations. ...She has captured the spirit of our view of the world, in which all things are connected and there is no distance between souls, alive or passed over, which cannot be bridged. We believe that *mana*, or life force, flows through the universe, and that all things have a voice ... even our dreams."

A general word for dreaming in Hawaiian is *moe'uhane*. It is usually translated as soul sleep and understood as night experiences of the soul. But rather than sleep, spirits roamed through the nights of old Hawaii and had great adventures in dreams. During soul sleep, relationships were sustained and the people received messages of guidance from the gods, deified ancestors and awaiku (angels).

> "Dreaming is when soul wakes up and goes traveling. You may fly across the water in your body of wind following the drumming of the waves to spend the night with your dream lover. Even goddesses do this."
>
> \- Roger Moss
> *Moe'uhane: Island Dreaming*

Discipline: Modern Dream Practice

My extensive dream research, *Wake Up To Dreaming* (2014), demonstrates that the soul experiences are revealed with discernment and practice. The discovery process in dream awareness is important to the waking mind and is a very empowering journey into the awareness of the self. A dream is like a mirror, in which you can see yourself as you really are or from another angle, which reflects vital information to you. A dream does not tell you what to do; rather it reveals to you what you *are* doing, what you *were* doing and the potential of what you *will be* doing. The meaningful message is derived from assessing the alternate perspective it has illustrated. When faced with a confusing dream riddle, don't give up. Its revelation is always pitched at a level just within reach of understanding, yet always a little bit beyond your total comprehension. That's why dreams portray the hidden truth that presents a challenge to discover all the facets of its revelations. The purpose is to broaden your mind and lead to what now becomes within your awareness. It is a part of your reality framework and it is a dramatic unfolding process, which brings information at a level of transformation that also expands your soul growth. Not only is dream analysis a deliberate and comprehensive self-revelation, it also is a tool of shamanic service. There are disclosures of the night called *ho'ike na ka po* in Hawaiian that carry the power of prophecy. It is one of the most exciting of dreams because it supplies information to the dreamer that is unknown to the conscious mind. Some of my dreams are solely in the form of a written document that I simply read and can record upon waking. The straight-up dreams (*moe pi'i pololei*) usually carry a very clear message. The revelatory dream is one of the most common dreams we have, although most people do not take time to learn the message it conveys. This is my story about a most profound and accurate revelatory dream series:

> "I met with a man and his secretary. The man headed an Arizona non-profit organization that had just announced receiving a million-dollar donation. They wanted me to be the Controller and Senior Pastor. My job would be to organize both the financial and spiritual aspects of the project. After deliberating with them before I went to bed, I asked God to give me a dream that would show me the situation in a different way. To my surprise, that night, my dream revealed a scene of the man and his secretary handing me a baby dressed in a smelly, wet night sleeper. This gave me the opportunity to question them about how long the company had been neglected and gave me a chance to find out why they wanted me to change their baby (project) that they were unwilling to care for properly. During my stay, each morning, I discussed issues I had dreamed about the night before. My dreams, during this trip, gave me vital information that contributed to what I needed to know about the organization."

This dreaming way of gathering practical information is available to anyone who will devote the time to learn the dreaming skills. However, many people trivialize or disregard dreams. The wise person investigates and discovers how to apply dream disclosures, which could be critical to their life. To integrate and honor the revelations, you must act upon the message within them. Once you develop your revelatory dream capacity, you may be ready to develop a new way to dream your life into existence.

Discipline: A New Way to Dream Life

Use the ancient Hawaiian belief that life starts when you go to sleep at night as a new way to dream life. Employ Haipule shortly before going to sleep each night. Ask your Divine Source to help you create your perfect life. Decide upon what you want to have happen the next day. Tell yourself to live it fully while you sleep and resolve to gather mana to use in physical form. Reinforce to yourself to actually live the life you want as you sleep. When you awaken, get up and live what you have created spiritually in the dream the night before. At the end of day, review what has happened in your life. At night, modify or change instructions to yourself to boldly live the life you want spiritually before you wake up. Work with your inner guidance to create life in this new shamanic way. Each night, repeat your new dream directives. Use pule (prayer). Utilize the time between sleeping and waking to anchor and encode the perfect life you have dreamed. Whether you remember your dream or not, this is a new way to dream life and live your life.

Discipline: Using Realities for Dream Interpretation

Another way to work with your dreams is to decide upon a focus each night. When you awaken, be empowered by viewing your dreams in each level of reality. Interpret each dream episode in the physical, psychic, symbolic, merging oneness and dream realities. Coordinate and compare your daytime experiences with your nighttime revelations. Listen to your inner dialogue and develop a new relationship with the expression of your Self in the outer world using realities for dream interpretation.

Chapter 13. The Halau: Angels, Guides & Ancestors

The Halau Guardians

The Halau Guardians (angels, guides and ancestors) are the spiritual support, which you might relate to as angelic or sacred beings that are here to help. These Spirits serve as links (aka cords) to the great Source that dreamed everything into existence. The paradox is that the Source lives and operates within and through each person and everything; yet we have forgotten our own connection. All can connect to the internal guidance system of the Hawaiian Halau. However, for the shaman, it is vital to consciously maintain a relationship with their spiritual helpers because they receive instructions and information to help them and those they serve. The spiritual Halau is a hierarchy of spiritual energy and support. In *Wise Secrets of Aloha* (3-4), Kahuna Harry Jim and Rev. Garnette Arledge explain:

> "The Halau can be defined as the continuum's comfort zone where we can learn. The Halau is all forces for good gathering to help us learn. The Halau guardians are multidimensional beings who support healing. When you enter the Halau, elders or guardians on the esoteric plane gather to meet you on this plane."

In communicating with the Halau, they come to you. You do not have to go anywhere other than to be present. It does not require beating of drums or other forms of induced trance-like states; it does require simplicity and sincerity. To fully understand the human evolution and to absorb the energy relates to the cooperation of humans and guardian spirits, angels, guides and ancestors. These are intermediaries who serve as emissaries to the higher realms of consciousness between humans and higher intelligences. Allow what influences you to come from the spiritually evolved Spirit teachers, which over time attune to higher and higher levels of consciousness vibration.

The Halau is a comfort zone for receiving inspiration, support and source of learning. The term is usually used to indicate a school of hula in Hawaii. The power of the Hawaiian word used here can be understood in the knowledge that the ancient Halau is an energy field. It is all forces for good that is generated by the esoteric energy, whether in body as in the energy field hula dancers generate, or spirit helpers who are not in body, who create an energy field of Spirit helpers.

Learning to work with the Halau is an important facet of Kupua mystical development. Professional psychic readers, mediums and healers who are in touch with their angels, guides and ancestors know the connection the Halau provides. Connection is a normal and natural occurrence. Everyone has the ability to connect in this wisdom space. You can develop expanded consciousness and establish a working relationship with higher consciousness if this is your intention. In *Wise Secrets of Aloha* (4) Kahuna Harry Uhane Jim provides instruction:

> "Thus, entering the Halau (the esoteric field for creating knowledge) is about expanding skills, empowering accuracy, and abundantly manifesting the healing ability by engaging with emotions. Persons ill in the body would come to the Kahuna for total wellness. We now call that holistic healing."

The ancient secrets may be revealed through investigation in the Halau, both physical and etheric. Your connection may also be reinforced through past life regression. Many tap into knowledge held genetically within their DNA and psyche.

Awaiku – Hawaiian Angels

Although angels are also a part of the Halau group, they are a specific group within the Halau that people are readily open to their communication and accept help from them. The angelic realm is a special connection in cultures all over the world, and they are trusted to give loving and gentle support to all. The awaiku are similar to Western concepts of angels, which are considered to be powerful, without the limitations of bodies and they are said to be able to fulfill wishes. If you lose contact with Divine Source, it is the awaiku who assist you to rebuild these connections. What is a little different with the Hawaiian awaiku is their relationship with the ancestors and agreement to work in the oneness together for the benefit of humanity. In this regard, you must discover your own position in the hierarchy. You may first need to reestablish and cleanse (*kala*) your connections with your dead ancestors, who assist to make pono with all. To understand awaiku is to understand more about the spirituality of the people and many of their beliefs that developed through the Kumulipo and I'O.

According to Kumu Miriam Baker of Ka'u, Big Island, there was never a time without awaiku. They were created at the beginning of creation, the dawn of Kumulipo manifesting within the infinite potential of a primeval god-energy. Aunty Miriam was known as the Angel Lady and authored *Our Angels and Our Mysteries*. She said that awaiku could be your most advanced teachers and your most naïve students. According to Kahuna Jim, what Miriam Baker taught was the many different ways that angels and spirit guides communicate. Everyone has the capability of being in touch with awaiku depending upon the intention set to work with the higher powers when you:

- Talk with loved ones who are deceased
- Cultivate visions
- Trust your intuitions
- Honor memories and experiences
- Be aware of recognizable symbols, images, and dreams
- Learn the Universal laws of Spirit and human dynamics
- Establish partnering relationships

Interpreting angel messages may not be easy at first because you may doubt or be tempted to add your own words or distort meaning unknowingly. With patience, you learn ways to transmit the purity and truth of the message.

> "The awaiku watch over the righteous of the earth. They shield the just and righteous children of Kane from injustice and deviltry at the hands of the unrighteous... The awaiku pour out Kane's love to the faithful, who look up to him for their blessings and are the messengers of man and God... healing angels who assist the Kahuna lapa'au by causing Divine healing power to flow from above to flow into these spiritual healers, giving them the power to cure their patients."
>
> - Julius Rodman, *Leinani Melville's Esoteric Hawaiian Dictionary (16-17)*

Ka Ho'omana'o ana no means the causing of empowerment through the spiritual teachings at the heart of Hawaiian spirituality. In the history of the teachings, we reconnect with the remembrances that are most valued. Notice the thread of ho'omana in Hawaiian spirituality. The support system of consciousness is all about self-empowerment (that comes from the Divine within). We are oneness in the consciousness we all share. The controlling conscious mind must learn this truth.

Spirit - Angels, Guides and Ancestors

> "With spirit, all things are possible, though man tends to easily disagree, and rightly so since man's mind is not familiar to possibilities, as it is to the impossibilities. And so it will take consistent mental re-enforcements to reconnect to truth and spirit realities."
>
> - Mahealani Kuamo'o-Henery

In Hawaiian thinking there is no death, just "changing address" from human to spirit form. It is a shedding of the physical body and represents new beginnings that may include serving as a spiritual guide on the other side. There is no difference in those who lived before, those living now or those who will live in the future... Consciousness includes all in the oneness of the present. In the separateness of today's beliefs, our spirit angels, guides and ancestors remind us that all souls have and are a spark of the Divine God/I'O.

For Hawaiians, communication continues between the living and the dead during dreams, prayer, by kilokilo (divination), or simply by casual conversation in thoughts as it does for many people around the world. Along with ancestors and gods, spirits are part of the Hawaiian life. Hawaiian writings *Ku Poʻe Kahiko: The People of Old*, the combined work of Kamakau, Samuel Manaiakalani, Mary Kawena Pukui, Dorothy B. Barrère and translated by Mary Kawena Pukui:

> "There are many kinds of spirits that help for good and many that aid in evil. Some lie and deceive, and some are truthful. ...It is a wonderful thing how the spirits (*uhane*) of the dead and the 'angels' (*anela*) of the ʻaumakua can possess living persons. Nothing is impossible to god-spirits, *akua*."

William Stead said that knowledge of the continuity of life after physical death makes life before death more meaningful. Knowing that life is eternal puts our life here in the material world in perspective. Spiritualism is a pathway of our spirit, a philosophy for living, not in the spirit world or the afterlife but living here and now. In the *Outline of Kahuna Lessons*, Daddy Bray said:

> "Without faith in the continuity of life through the ancestors and our descendants a breakdown in the relations between youth and elder would occur... The means by which this breach could be repaired: with the love and understanding found in a reconnection to the Path of Aloha."

Communication with Spirit is called Spiritualism, which is also a dialogue with your soul and a lifelong dialogue with the Divine. Through communication with Spirit, we are directly in touch with the ancients who give instructions connected to life today. Spiritual medium Gordon Higgins said that we should learn about our own spirit before trying to make links with other spirits. In *Great Moments of Modern Mediumship*, Maxine Meilleur quotes his poem *Touch The Spirit Within:*

> "Before you can touch the Spirit, you must find it within yourself. For all truth, all knowledge and all loving must first be found within oneself.
> The Spirit can never touch you, and bring Love and Peace within your being and from your being, until you have found it for yourself.
> And before you can build a picture of love from Spirit, you must learn to find it in this life.
> Always prepare yourself as a channel for Spirit. Stand there with Love radiating from you. Then God will touch you.
> So, be still, be present with yourself, be present with your soul and your inner divinity."

Communications with the Ancestors

My story of communication with the angels, guides and ancestors began when I first opened to communications with Spirit. In the 1950's, my pastor encouraged me to allow the Holy Spirit to speak through me when testifying to individuals. I tried it. Before it was time to witness to someone, I would pray, "God, please speak through me." Not only did it help me overcome my feeling of inadequacy, but it also seemed to help those with whom I spoke. It was considered to be a *Gift of the Spirit*, which I later used when I was 17 in my position as Minister of Music. Later in life, this gift kept "slipping out" during counseling sessions. So, in 1982, I began taking classes through a Spiritualist healing and mediumship program to become a disciplined messenger of Spirit. Gaining self-control in this ability led to communications from personalities such as Jesus, Uli, other spiritual messengers, and special connection with my mother. As I became more comfortable with communion with Spirit, I connected with the energies of those who came to assist Earth, known as the Lemurian Council. In conscious trance, I found myself channeling the words and hula movement of consciousness. Uli, the mother of Mu became a teacher and mentor who spoke and danced hula through me in public meetings. Through the Halau, I experienced a deep connection with Lemuria and awakened to remembrances, which I explained in the booklet, *Lemuria Calling*. The Ancient Ones knew and functioned in the state of expanded awareness. I experienced a very mystically enhancing energy communication:

> "...Speaking of a source of loving energy, which appears in soft and gentle radiating light... nudging humanity to explore the oneness of the Light. It whispers, *Remember who you are.*"

What I now know was a Halau experience, became a deepening of my mediumistic experience with the ancestors, angels, and guides. It was an introduction to my soul-lineage of Hawaiian Shamanism. My mind sought confirmation from outside this inner connection. Therefore, I researched a physical connection with the mysteries. Hawaii was the physical link to my Spirit source. When I studied with Serge Kahili King, the Hawaiian god, Kanaloa, came in immediately to lead with his tutelage and to an association with one of his direct descendants. The blessings I received from the mystical Hawaiian Spirit Halau continue to bless me today.

Old Hawaiians believed that angels, guides, and ancestors could take possession of a person's body. I experienced this as I addressed the 100th Anniversary of the Universal Church of the Master. As in previous conscious trance states, when I began to speak, I could sense a deepening in my alpha brain activity and felt the presence of the Holy Spirit. I allowed the words and body movements to be generated and controlled from my Spirit guide. What I was not prepared for was the total movement of my body dancing off the stage where no stairs existed. As I glided off the platform, I felt a twinge of panic from my observing conscious mind. Uli whispered to me, "Don't worry." So, I took a deeper breath, relaxed, and trusted. I felt myself land gracefully as I continued dancing through the auditorium under Spirit control. Thankfully, upon returning to the stage, Spirit did use the stairs. While many stories of a discarnate Spirit-possession tell of an involuntary and negative experience, my experience has always been a cooperative voluntary process to fulfill a spiritual mission.

Communication between the living and the dead is a reality for the Hawaiians and the professionally trained medium. Every time we remember some person, place or thing, we are in touch with someone or a group (the Halau). We are in communication just as if we are sitting in the same room. Actually, we *are* in the same energy, which registers subtle vibrations that most people miss. The impressions are so slight that it is easy to dismiss the seemingly insignificant vibrations. We may choose to ignore these faint impressions, or we can investigate and trust our senses that we are somehow in communication with our loved ones; the choice is ours. I have benefited greatly from Spirit communication while writing this book. I received impressions in response to some questions, which formed in my mind. The more questions I pondered, the stronger I felt the communications until a most amazing experience unfolded. I am grateful to have been tutored by Kahuna Kupua Mystics, other Kahuna traditions, and several Masters who are presently incarnated.

> "To Hawaiians, we are only a part of life on earth, a part of God's magnificent creation in the vast darkness of the universe. We respect all life, for they are our ancestors personified. We hold tenderly our aloha to our 'uhane families and ancestors who are the na pua of this 'aina. We thank God, Our Almighty Creator, for all that nurtures us from the land and sea. But most of all, we know our inherited role as Kahu (caretakers) of God's majestic creation and protectors of our ancestors 'uhane. It is a responsibility that we take with great humbleness and sincerity."
>
> - Kahuna Kuhikuhi Pu'uone
> *The Natural World And Our Hawaiian Spirituality (1996)*

Chapter 14. Work of the Modern Shaman

"What lies before us and what lies behind us are small matters compared to what lies within us. And when we bring what is within out into the world, miracles happen."

- Ralph Waldo Emerson

The modern shaman is a person who has dedicated him or herself to bring what is within, out into the world to make love-miracles happen. Much is said about the ability a shaman must have to understand all levels of reality and function in all phases of energy for self and society. However, at the core of the work is the ability to be in the highest of consciousness, sustain it, interact with it and serve those who function in the state of drama and trauma existing in the density of the world. This devotion is a commitment to connect and transmit the energy of the Divine in assisting people to be all that they can be.

The great work in the contemporary world, as it was in ancient times, is found in the ability to live from the highest state of integrity. Within the high calling of the shaman, as conveyed in the Hawaiian pantheon and deities of all religions, the work in consciousness is evident worldwide. Shamanic service always conveys the mission to become impervious to lower consciousness influences. Individuals are called to overcome the density held by humanity and at the same time, to serve in and become a bridge between the chaos of the material world and the spiritual realm to bring healing and transformation.

The Shaman Mask

In Hawaiian Shamanism, the commitment of the ancient ones to function in higher consciousness is called *Wearing the Shaman Mask*.

"The kapa and gourd assisted him in maintaining the state of total integrity, by providing a physical form to 'contain' the spiritual energies. It also provided a 'face' to allow the other people to 'see' the spiritually balanced warrior."

– Aunty Laura Kealoha Yardley
Empowerment Weekend January 1999

Shaman Mask

The Gourd Mask Denotes a State of Integrity

Wearing the Shaman Mask (an actual physical gourd helmet) is the metaphysical opposite of a mask. This Shaman Mask does not hide or conceal the person for any reason; instead it signifies and advertises the fact that he or she has become invisible. It is a commitment by the wearer to make their spiritual presence available to others who remain in an ordinary state of consciousness. Adorned with a sedge crest, it signified the growth from the lowliest to the highest of plants. When you earn the right to wear the gourd mask, you have learned to truly serve humanity in an extraordinary way. In modern times, it is an opportunity to be in the state of highest integrity, being separate from the chaos of the world as you do your work. In practice, it provides mana for you to function as *"Your Real Spirit Self"* in pono. This is the mission and the great work of the shaman.

Living Pono

Living pono is a Hawaiian principle of consistently living in the highest integrity of rightness, harmony and balance with all. It is about *thinking pono* and contributing toward positive outcomes for the whole. The mission calls for self-evaluation and self-monitoring of your beliefs, values and your ability to act in pono behavior. The responsibility of the dedicated shaman is found in the ability to live, convey love and teach pono. Living pono means living with a conscious decision to do the right thing in terms of yourself, others and the environment. Pono is functioning from the place of truth. In essence, every action in the life and service of the shaman is either pono or not. When you have earned the right to wear the shamans' mask, you have learned to operate from your spiritual center, the place of pure love, where your Divine presence can create pono. This is deeply profound; it is purity in its most loving form.

The Practice of Pono - Ka Hana Pono

Ka Hana Pono means to be in harmony with reality. To understand the empowerment, look to the inner meanings. Hana means work. It comes from the Hawaiian words *ha* meaning breath and *na*, plural form, which means an active centered calmness. Hana also means many breaths. Gratitude, combined with intention is a portal to right action; it is an automatic activator of pono, and it aligns with your Spirit greatness. The moment you feel gratitude, you are in pono and ready to practice pono. The moment you stop practicing the intention of pono you are in density. The goal is to expand your intention into a lifetime of practicing pono.

Ike Pono means to know what is right. Practicing pono is not only what is right, but it means to *do* what is right. Pono evaluates truth in behavior. The evidence of right action asks one simple question, "*Is your action pono or not?*" A shaman must demonstrate perfect relationship with the creative energy of the universe. If you want to create pono, then you must <u>be</u> pono and <u>act</u> in pono (loving action) in all areas of interaction. Kupono is a process to make things right from within. Kupono infuses mana to empower your right, desire, will and the power within. It uses a detailed mental rehearsal combined with physical posturing to change your relationship within yourself. The powerful process manifests an empowerment culminating in right action.

Ho'oponopono Basics

Ho'oponopono is the art and practice of life balance including harmony of the selves and with all things (making things right).

In the Hawaiian language ho'oponopono means to make right with people and the ancestors. It also means to make ready as a canoe paddler prepares to catch a wave. It is not always hurt and disappointment that need to be healed, it is also preparation for living in right relationship. Ho'oponopono teaches how the differences and uncertainties within the self provide a rich opportunity to recognize the reality of life and the potential to live in higher consciousness through all of life's challenges.

Ho'oponopono - Achieving Right Action

Ho'o: to cause something to happen
Pono: in alignment and balance with all things
Ponopono: using pono twice adds mana to create perfection in our behavior and with all things

The practice of ho'oponopono grows out of the traditions that share common values of aloha conduct, of the personal self and Aumakua (God), and with ohana (family) cooperation. Kupuna Nana Veary wrote that when any of the children in her family fell ill, her grandmother would ask the parents, "What have you done?" They believed that healing could come only with complete forgiveness of the whole family. To understand ho'oponopono, my first physical Hawaiian teacher Kumu Frank Kawaikapuokalani Hewett, taught this Hawaiian thinking:

1. One must first understand the word *Pono* and traditions within the Hawaiian culture.
2. Pono in relationship to the Natural Order.
3. Pono in relationship to God, Ancestor worship, the environment and to Man.
4. Pono and responsibility.
5. Pono and forgiveness.
6. Pono and genealogy.
7. Pono and being connected.
8. Pono and past life.
9. Pono and present life.
10. Pono and future life.

When you investigate the points of Kumu Hewett, you will awaken to the Hawaiian way of aloha and understand the meaning of ho'oponopono as it is meant by Hawaiian traditions to assist yourself and others. I invite you to make the study of ho'oponopono from all these perspectives to discover what it intrinsically entails. What is presented just scratches the surface of understanding how to live in the pono loving relationship with yourself and others, by describing ho'oponopono from the various vantage points. The group participation raises the consciousness of each person as they heal injuries and harmonize relationships, forming a greater bond of love and understanding with each other.

Ho'oponopono Philosophy - Catalyst to Change

If something disturbs you, disharmony is felt within; there is a conflict of belief somewhere. If there is conflict within, there is conflict without. Ho'oponopono must be made within yourself to have restoration and have pono action without. Contained in the Spirit of Aloha and its practice is the sense that if harmony is disrupted, a person must have the courage to ask forgiveness of themselves and must extend it to others. Completing the ho'oponopono process from the aloha the shaman brings, is the catalyst for amazing change. The practice is an acknowledgement of a problem, identifying the action of the problem and honestly looking on all sides at its internal roots. The necessary healing steps include making a definite decision to forgive, as well as a commitment to let go of the past hurt or damage. It may involve admitting to inappropriate words, thoughts, or actions. When this is done, a deep sense from within the individual arises when right relationship is restored.

Na kala - The Fortune of Forgiveness

The Hawaiian concept of forgiveness is different from the Western cultural approach in that the goal is to restore pono. Thus, forgiveness to restore true pono (loving alignment and right action) does not happen when the words of forgiveness occur; it happens when you forgive and let go. Kala was an expression used when the ancients prayed to their gods for forgiveness. Hawaiian values include a profound code of forgiveness. They believe that when you forgive others, you are also forgiving yourself. Kala means to untie, unbind and set free. The person, group or nation to whom the wrongdoer is indebted frees themselves and others of the karmic debt or wrongdoing. In unbinding attachments to past wrongs by making right the future, the wrong does not exist anymore. Etua Lopez, Kumu Hula (hula teacher), always says:

> "You forgive. You forget the incident. You remember only the learning. You remember what it is that you need to do in order to create your universe the way that you want."

The Family/Group Ho'oponopono Process

The *haku* (arbitrator) is chosen to facilitate ho'oponopono to make it right. Each person must be sincere in their desire and commitment to resolve differences. All must agree to talk freely, until all sides are heard and understood abiding by the rules of this process:

1. Participate fully in the process.
2. Tell your own truth.
3. Love each other.
4. Restore your connection to the Spirit of Aloha.
5. Hold confidential everything that takes place in the process.

To be effective, there must be a unified force, a pooling of mana (energy, strength) directed toward a positive goal. Steps to reconcile differences is opportunity to restore what was destroyed by the prior unloving, intentional or thoughtless actions. The guidelines are:

Ho'oponopono Traditional Group Conflict Resolution

1. Prayer: *Pule Wehe* – Call in spiritual power and guidance
2. Clarify the situation: *Kukulu Kamahana* - Identify problem
3. State the transgression: *Hala*
4. Discussion: M*ahiki* - Unravel the problem
5. Identify hurtful entanglements: *Hihia*
6. Share thoughts and feelings: *Mana'o*
7. Confession: *Mihi* – repent, apologize, forgive completely
8. Release and make amends: *Kala* – release, untie, unbind
9. Clear and cut off problems: *Oki*
10. Restore Aloha: *Pani* – make amends/perfect relationships
11. Closing Prayer: *Pule Ho'opau* – Appreciation, Gratitude
12. Celebrate: *Pa'ina* - Establish joyful harmonies

Ho'oponopono involves self-reflection to evaluate personal behavior and acknowledge unfair or hurtful interactions. Prayers, meditation and spiritual guidance help solve problems. Once harmony and balance is restored, loving action empowers and transforms through those who live by this empowering code. In the shifting consciousness today, humanity seeks the way of pono restoration and stability. The practice of ho'oponopono continues to be an important work of the modern shaman.

The Internalizing Practice of Ho'oponopono

Morrnah Nalamaku Simeona, Hawaiian Kahuna Lapa'au healer, refined the subtleties and application of ho'oponopono. She presented a new form of resolution-forgiveness healing that began a movement, which has touched the lives of people globally. At the root of the personal healing formula is this restorative principle:

> "We can appeal to Divinity who knows our personal blueprint, for healing of all thoughts and memories that are holding us back at this time ...It is a matter of going beyond traditional means of accessing knowledge about ourselves."

The healing process includes connecting one's soul with the Divine. The form of this personal ho'oponopono restoration involves four phrases, which can be repeated to yourself in any order. This establishes a higher consciousness energy:

Hawaiian Words	English Meaning
Kala'ana	I am sorry
E Kala Mai Ia 'Au	Please forgive me
Mahalo Nui Loa	Thank you
Aloha No Wau 'Ia 'Oe	I love you

The words are to be said over and over, to restore and program the subconscious mind in the ways of aloha and pono. A person connects her or his own inner Light with the Light of Source. Over time, discordant patterns in the subconscious (stones in your Sacred Bowl of Light) dissolve and by forgiving the parts within that hold those patterns, the person's outer world regains balance and harmony. We can maintain pono through the use of ho'oponopono restorative practices. Each person must figure out his or her own practice of pono and what to do to restore it if it is lost. It is the responsibility of each person to bridge the gap of known and hidden truths of love and right relationships.

The Carriers of the Light

The Carriers of the Light (those who serve as the transporters of Inner Light to other souls) are waking up to the Hawaiian knowledge that they carry the Bowl of Light within themselves. As depicted on the cover, there is a Shaman Star, the spiritual light through which we are, that shines from within each person. Others can recognize the mana even though the wearer who is seeking to find it does not know the star shines from within.

You might not be physically born Hawaiian in this lifetime, but be a carrier of the Light. Today, more people are awakening to the hidden knowledge and honor their self-greatness. Each Light carrier must discover these truths and accept the mission to walk up the mountain, protecting their aloha as they tend and carry the Light. The life of the Carrier is filled with opportunity for spiritual growth every day. This insures that mana is present in their personal and collective Community Bowl of Light. The work of Hawaiian shamanism today is to make known the influence of the Upper Light. Knowingly carry the Light, the force of life, and create the proper environment to develop spiritually. Bridge the density gap using the mana of pure aloha from an awakened heart and mind. When a stone appears, let go of it so that the natural state of ho'oponopono is once again restored to you. Kahu Brandt gave us this insight:

> "All sacred traditions must evolve to meet the context and realities of modern day life for them to stay relevant. In this way, the sacred trust that has been

passed to us will find a strong home in this and the next generation."

Modern shaman carry the Light to embody aloha as a way of being, and commit to a lifestyle of wise and compassionate living. When someone gets angry with you, observe the behavior in you that caused the reaction in him or her. Take full responsibility for your part. That's the portion you can apologize for, and change your behavior. This restores pono, resulting in harmony and balance in yourself. As you grow in pono, you build bridges of higher consciousness in yourself and others, which establishes healing throughout your ministerial service. This vision is carried by Serge King and is reflected in the *Urban Shaman* (34):

> "Hawaiian shamanism and the Spirit of Aloha on which it is based represent a way of life with great value for all of humanity. It is a coming together time for all, and the best use of all shamanism, urban and otherwise, would be for the cause of peace, inner and outer. As an old Hawaiian proverb says: *He ali'i ka la'i, he haku na ke aloha* (Peace is a chief, the lord of love). May peace and love be our guide and our purpose as we work on healing the world today."

Do not let the values of the Hawaiian heritage slip into the night to lie dormant. Take the inspiration of the sacred traditions and add to them from deep within your own soul. Adopt the teachings of higher consciousness and the life it establishes into the world around you wrapped in the goals of your own life's mission. When this is done, the modern shaman has a way of thinking and acting that defies boundaries and limitations, while remaining linked with the ancients.

Reconcile the pressures of modern life to be in touch with the core truths you have come to live. Humanity is gifted with the Light coding perfectly intact. It is hidden deep within the collective consciousness that is remembered now. There are no accidents, only the timeless and opportune moments to experience the desires that each person spiritually, physically, and energetically seek to create and manifest each in his or her own way. The world needs the influence of your Bowl of Light that transforms with aloha, lokahi, and pono in all things through oneness. When you tend and share your Light, you have transcended the need to wear a shaman mask. It is an emergence of the Light within your heart that *must* be shared with the world. Heed Kahuna Daddy Bray's invitation:

> "Come forward, be in unity and harmony with your real self, God, and mankind. Be honest, truthful, patient, kind to all forms of life, and humble."

This is the time of the re-emergence of shaman values. It is an opening to accept and experience your own self-greatness in the way of aloha. You too, can love all that you see with humility, live all that you feel with reverence, and use all your talents and abilities with discipline. It is a path to demonstrate who you are in self-mastery and in service to humanity, which offers a way to always honor the Divine mysteries you find in all traditions. Therefore, be attentive to the mystery in every experience; it will mean that you will give attention to what you do not know. Instead of approaching the world with your known conclusions, become receptive to more of what is actually here. More of the mystery of life, in the old ways, will be revealed as you find yourself in a state of constant discovery.

Live Aloha - Love, Honor, and Respect All

The true meaning of aloha is to love, honor, and respect everyone. Living aloha in a modern world where you are physically away from nature and Hawaiian thinking is challenging. However, it presents possibilities to live with mindfulness and intention with other Light bearers as you move forward with vision. The invitation is not to live in the past, nor is it to grow without the roots. It is to be motivated with purpose as you gather the love and wisdom of the ancestors to bring the best of it into an ever-evolving world. Recently I learned about the true story of a young Hawaiian girl depicted in the short film *A Place in the Middle* by the Emmy Award-winning filmmaker, Dean Hamer that has been excerpted for the *Perspectives for a Diverse America* anthology. The video helps young people see the value of inclusion and tolerance in demonstrating the deeper meaning of aloha. Although the video is geared to teach school children, the message in the beliefs is at the heart of Hawaiian Shamanism. May we all pledge to live aloha to bring peace and healing to our world. This is the pledge:

The Pledge of Aloha

I believe that every person has a role in society, and deserves to be included and treated with respect in their family, school, and community.

I believe that every person should be free to express what is truly in their heart and mind, whether male, female, or in the middle.

I believe that every person should be able to practice their cultural traditions, and to know and perpetuate the wisdom of their ancestors for future generations.

I believe these values are embodied in aloha: love, honor, and respect for all.

Therefore, I pledge to live aloha in everything I do, and to inspire people of all ages to do the same.

Those who will faithfully follow the footsteps of the Masters will walk the path that can lead to a fulfilling relationship with humanity and experience greater joy in accepting the mystical gift of the Masters. Once a commitment is made to become a vital part of the spiritual hierarchy, it includes discovering what it is that you are meant to bring into this world. You may find that you are the bridge to lead to the deeper levels of awareness. Hence, do not fear to go beyond what you already know. As you take steps to reach the top of the mountain, your vision will be clarified and refined, for the revelation itself permeates all, as it too evolves. This may be your opportunity to accept the gift of the shaman shoes and find the secrets, which empower and change your life.

Ho'o! - Make it happen!

Pule Ho'opau – Closing Ritual

Po'e Au'makua. Our Spirit Family, beloved Ancestors, Guides, and Teachers.

Mahalo. We thank you for your presence and your support in our work each day. Thank you for the gift of your Divine wisdom. May we go forth in this work and use it wisely.

Thank you for providing the practice of Kupua Ancient traditions so we may become all that we have the potential to be. Thank you for providing us tools so we may continue to work on self-balance and integration of our selves. We love you and thank you deeply. The circle of blessings continues to spiral outward.

We live in Aloha and Pono. We walk in Aloha and Lokahi, in harmony and balance to bring wholeness to ourselves and assist others.

E Aloha Mana Pono.
Blessings of Love, Empowerment and Loving Right Action.

Amama ua noa.
The prayer is complete.

Mahalo, Mahalo, Mahalo.
Thank you. Thank you. Thank you.
May the breath of life stay with you.

Acknowledgement

Contributions from the Carriers of the Light

Today, the Light of the Carriers extends globally. It permeates the consciousness of all people. Once touched by the Light, you become a member of the people of the Light. The Light Carrier Ohana extends to the known and unknown carriers as well. Its aka carries the Light to shine in all corners, no matter how dark it may seem to be. Teachers of the Light, with whom Dr. Phelan studied in person and through books, tapes, and Spirit communications are deeply entwined within her. These are the basis for this work and therefore it may also touch you deeply if you accept their esoteric connection. When the ancient way of life changed by influences of density, as it did in all parts of the world, Hawaiian mystical knowledge and its ho'omana was hidden by the choice of the many devoted Light Carriers. Through efforts of some outstanding individuals, the light still shines and is shared and preserved with the world community through living its truth.

One exceptional leader who extended his Light was Po'oKahuna Pule Lanakilakahuokalani Brandt, consecrated priest of Mo'o Lono order (1924–2005). As a lifetime Hawaiian religionist and fluent Hawaiian dialect speaker, Kahu served as language, tradition and spiritual consultant to Hawaiian publications, Leinani Melville Jones, (*Children of the Rainbow* and the *Esoteric Hawaiian Dictionary*) and huna author Max Freedom Long (*Secret Science Behind Miracles*). As a Hawaiian mysteries scholar, beloved Lanakila was dedicated to teaching the methods of *Ke Oihaa Kahiko* (the ancient priesthood) and taught thousands of non-Hawaiians the traditions of Ho'omana Kahiko to create a sacred living aka bridge between the gods and people.

Through studies with Kumu Frank Kawaikapuokalani Hewitt, at various times since the early 1980's, it was Dr. Phelan's first introduction to the ancient Hawaiian ways. Kumu Hula (hula master), Frank perpetuates the ancient mana in his teaching and through sacred hula; his ability to channel Spirit is superb and continues to touch hearts around the world.

Acknowledgement

Aunty Laura Kealoha Yardley, Ph.D., connecting to the ancestors through the legacy of Lemuria, extended shaman training to non-Hawaiians in programs and mentoring. Dr. Yardley connects with the old ways through her grandmother Puna's wisdom along with the teaching of other Kahuna from the islands. *The Heart of Huna* is a primer to learn the Hawaiian beliefs of lokahi (unity), mihi (forgiveness), ohana (family), and kala (cleansing) that touches people deeply.

Of contemporary visionaries since late 1960, one of the most prolific of the messengers is Dr. Serge Kahili King, Ph.D., as he continues to teach and write about the aspects of the Kahuna Kupua. From his perspective of the Order of Kane, the world is what you think it is and it is a reflection of your thoughts. There is emphasis on the integration of body, mind, and spirit for the purpose of self-mastery. He teaches that self-mastery is the key to mastery of life. Dr. King invites individuals to go through the door of knowledge that he opens and points them to grow in their own way through their own exploration. His worldwide organization connects the Western mind to the philosophies of the Kupua Shaman through contemporary understanding.

One of Dr. Phelan's teachers, Kumu Hula Susan Pa'iniu Floyd, author of *Magic Hands and Loving Heart*, provides profound and effective instruction of the Hawaiian way, which she lives. This knowledge is perpetuated in the higher consciousness of her authentic hula and ancient Hawaiian temple healing arts. Thousands of students are grateful recipients of the training of empowering Kino Mana modalities and Hawaiian philosophies that carry with them the dynamics of the Divine feminine. These are intrinsic to the messages from the ancients of Uli, Hawaiian priests, na kahuna and those who have graduated into Spirit.

Revered Hawaiian Kapuna Nana Veary, who authored *Change We Must,* was an embodiment of the true meaning of aloha. Upon her passing in the early 1980's, her spirit communicated clearly during the moving televised memorial service through the eulogy given by Richard Chamberlain. Her teaching of non-verbal communications was proof that communications with those in Spirit is real and in fact, happen every day.

Abraham Kawaii (transitioned 2004) of the Order of Olohe taught Kahuna sciences to non-Hawaiian students with the purpose of training them to be Kahuna. His legacy includes, but is not limited to, the ancient art of movement of consciousness. The work is now carried through his well-trained students. Kahu Abraham's profound ancient temple practices influenced Dr. King's work in Aloha International through the work of Kumu Hula Susan Pa'iniu Floyd. Kahu Kawaii's legacy is also carried through the work of fellow Kupua practitioner Wayne Kealohi Powell (Hawaiian Shamanic Bodywork).

Kahuna David Kaonohiokala Bray (1889-1968), was a Kahuna of the order of Kane who used a spiritual and integrative approach to Hawaiian mysticism. He authored *The Kahuna Religion of Hawaii* assisted by Douglas Low, which wonderfully outlines principles of spiritual development needed for service as a Po'o Kahuna. It is a playbook to bring you success in your Kahuna initiation progression. Today, from Spirit, he quickly responds to requests for help and will project ideas or whisper Hawaiian philosophical points of view.

The Halau Guardians (angels, guides and ancestors) have been a spiritual support and an important resource in expanding the scope of *Hawaiian Shamanism*. From the first to current contacts, all prove the continuity of life and that we are all one consciousness.

To all Carriers of the Light, for whom this book is written:

You are all brothers and sisters, known and unknown. Many have been teacher or student, friend or foe, lover and family from ancient times. Special mention is given to:

Michael Yee, Kahuna of the ocean as was Kanaloa; Rev. Melainah Yee, powerful Goddess of Mu and of Pele; Rev. Chris Reid, Goddess mother Dolphin queen, supreme in aina and sea; Rev. Rebecca Thompson, collaborator, modern Mystic and Merlin

ACKNOWLEDGEMENT

of old; Wisdom Woman Lynn Kaleihaunani Melena, ancient Kumu Hula; Jan Venturini, Multidimensional orchestrator of Divine guidance; Rev. Ronald E. McLain, B.Msc., Medicine Song and wise Shaman; and Rev. Carolyn V. Keyes, Aloha Collaborator and Flutist extraordinaire. To those esteemed fellow ministering peers world-wide and at CCL founded by Rev. Doti Boon assisted by the Rev. Corky Whitaker and Rev. Donna Zehner; friends, teachers, students and clients I serve; beloved husband, children, grand and great grandchildren, siblings, nieces, nephews; to all who agreed to be incarnated with me:

I love and appreciate each of you and the family legacy you are creating through yourself and your lineage. May you feel you are loved and accepted by all your family. You are each special souls to me, and valuable to the entire consciousness system of souls. Your consciousness supports and influences all. I honor you.

E ho'omaika'i O la'a kea me ke aloha pau ole
Blessings of sacred light and everlasting love

- Arlene, mother, et al

Bibliography

Baker, Miriam, *Our Angels and Our Mysteries* 1992, Self-Published Hawking Books, Lake Arrowhead, CA

Beckwith, Martha Warren, *Hawaiian Mythology* 1970, University of Hawaii Press, Honolulu, HI

Beckwith, Martha Warren, *Translation and Commentary, The Kumulipo: A Hawaiian Creation Chant*, American Folklore Society referenced at Ulukau: The Hawaiian Electronic Library

Berney, Charlotte, *Fundamentals of Hawaiian Mysticism* 2000, Crossing Press, Berkeley, CA

Brandt, Lanakila, *The Sacred Keys Of The Masters, Ho'omana Kahiko* 2003, Kahanahou Hawaiian Foundation, Hawaii, HI

Brandt, Lanakila, *Po'ohuna* 1997, Kahanahou Hawaiian Foundation, Hawaii, HI

Bray, David K, and Low, Douglas, *The Kahuna Religion of Hawaii* 1960, Borderland Sciences Research Foundation

Carter, Paul Milton, Ph.D., *Trance and Healing Instruction* 2009, Makawao, HI 96768

Calleman, Carl Johan, *Calendar: The Pyramid of Consciousness. Global Oneness.* The Global Oneness

Churchward, Col. James, *The Sacred Symbols of Mu* 1933, Ives Washburn, NY

Handy, ES Craighill, *Polynesian Religion* 1927, Bernice P Bishop Museum, Honolulu, HI

Holmes, Ernest Shurtleff, *The Science of Mind, Lesson 5: The Perfect Whole* 1926, at sacred-text.com. *The Science of Mind*

Jim, Harry Uhane, and Arledge, M.Div., Rev. Garnette, *Wise Secrets of Aloha: Learn and Live the Sacred Art of Lomilomi 2007*, Weiser, Conari

Johan, Carl, *Solving the Greatest Mystery of Our Time: The Mayan Calendar* 2000

BIBLIOGRAPHY

Kamakau, Samuel Manaiakalani; Mary Kawena Pukui, Dorothy B Barrère, *Ka Po'e Kahiko: The People of Old* 1964, translated by Mary Kawena Pukui, Bishop Museum Press

Kauka, Sabra, *Religions, Mythology, and Ritual*, Cultural Practitioner, Kauai, HI

King, Ph.D., Serge Kahili, *Kahuna Healing* 1979, Huna International, Malibu, CA

King, Ph.D., Serge Kahili, *Seeing Is Believing, The Four Worlds of a Shaman* Pamphlet, Aloha International, Kauai, Hi

King, Ph.D., Serge Kahili, *Urban Shaman* 1990, Fireside, Rockefeller Center, New York, NY 10020

Kumukahi Educators, *Kamehameha* 2017, Publishing, Honolulu, HI publishing@ksbe.edu

Lee, Pali Jae, Willis, Koko, *Tales From The Night Rainbow*, 1986, Night Rainbow Publishing Co., Honolulu, HI

Loebel-Fried, Caren *Hawaiian Legends of Dreams* 2005, University of Hawai'i Press, Honolulu, HI

Meadows, Kenneth, *Shamanic Spirit: A Practical Guide to Personal Fulfillment* 2004, Bear and Company, Rochester, VT

Meilleur, Maxine, *Great Moments of Modern Mediumship*, 2014 Saturday Night Press Publications, info@snppbooks.com

Melville (Jones), Leinani, *Children of the Rainbow: The Legends of Gods of Pre-Christian Hawaii* 1969, Theosophical Publishing House, Wheaton, IL

Melville (Jones), Leinani, *Esoteric Hawaiian Dictionary*, 1996 Reprint Heart of Huna, Mill Valley, CA

Phelan, Arlene, Ph.D., *Lemuria Calling 1991,* APA, Hayward, CA

Pukui, Mary Kawena and Elbert, Samuel, *Hawaiian Dictionary: Hawaiian-English English-Hawaiian* 1986, University of Hawaii Press, Honolulu, HI

Rodman, Julius Scammon, *Kahuna Sorcerers of Hawaii, Past and Present* 1979, Exposition Press, Hicksville, NY

Steiger, Brad, *Kahuna Magic* 1971, Para Books, Schiffer Publishing, Ltd., West Chester, PA

Underhill, Evelyn, *Practical Mysticism* 1914, Ariel Press, Columbus, OH

Veary, Nana, *Change We Must: My Spiritual Journey* 1990, Medicine Bear Publishing, Blue Hills, NJ

Wesselman, Hank, *Bowl of Light* 2011, Sounds True, Inc., Boulder, CO

Yardley, Laura Kealoha, Ph.D., *Heart of Huna* 1990, Advanced Neuro Dynamics, Honolulu, HI

Yardley, Laura Kealoha, Ph.D., *Heart of Huna Empowerment Weekend*, Santa Sabina, CA 1999, Heart of Huna Publication

About The Author

**Rev. Arlene Phelan, Ph.D.** is recognized internationally as a mystical Hawaiian Kupua Shaman and is listed with Aloha International Resource of Huna Teachers and Therapists – USA since 1995, in the categories of Teaching, Counseling, Lomi Lomi Massage and Kahi Loa Therapists. An ordained minister since 1984, Hawaiian Shamanism has been her special study with many Kahuna in Hawaii and in joyful practice.

Arlene was known as a global leader in the Hospitality Financial Technology Professionals HFTP (president 1983-84), 10 years of international board service, and as president of the San Francisco and South Florida area chapters. Her professional career as a Comptroller and Director of Finance led to establishing her own consulting business that offered financial, and hotel consulting. After ministerial ordination, Rev. Phelan led a church ministry with emphases on pastoral guidance and ministerial preparation. Her ministry expanded to include the practice and teaching of Hawaiian Shamanism and the ancient temple healing, as well as facilitating life path guidance.

Rev. Phelan earned her Doctor of Philosophy degree specializing in Metaphysical Counseling from the University of Sedona, Arizona. She is a member of the University Alumni Association, AMDA (American Metaphysical Doctors Association), and International Metaphysical Ministry Counseling Psychology Association.

In addition to *Hawaiian Shamanism, Secrets of the Modern Shaman*, Dr. Phelan has authored self-help books as personal and professional development tools. Publications are: *Lemuria Calling, The Presence and Power of Huna, The Dynamics of the Ministry, Ministerial Preparation Workbooks*, and the *Wake up to Dreaming Series*. Soon to be published are: *Life Path Destiny - Finding Your Imprint; Life Path Numbers - Discover Your Personal Power and Destiny Imprint;* the revised *Dynamics of the Ministry*.

Made in the USA
Columbia, SC
13 October 2018